ZONDERVAN

BIBLE STUDY GUIDE
SAMPLER

A taste of the bestselling Bible studies for small groups

ZONDERVAN™

GRAND RAPIDS, MICHIGAN 49530 USA

Contents

Foreword

As a small group or Bible study leader you have a significant ministry in God's church building up the body of Christ. This book has been designed specifically for you. Our hope is that this book will save you time and direct you to resources that will make your ministry even more effective and fun! We know you'd rather be spending your time studying God's word and caring for your group members rather than hunting for good ministry tools. At regular times during the year you look for new tools to use in your small group ministry. Usually it's a study guide that your group can use together. Other times it's a book to help with the challenges of small group ministry.

To make your life a little simpler we've gathered samples of the small group resources in Zondervan's portfolio into one convenient book. The books in this sampler are the work of experts in small group ministry and bible study. Review these resources on your own, and share them with your small group to determine the ones that will meet your group's needs.

Zondervan's mission is to be the leading Christian communications company meeting the needs of people with resources that glorify Jesus Christ and promote biblical principles. Zondervan Bible study tools have met the needs of millions of small group members over the years.

Please let us know if they meet your needs. How did they meet your needs? Did your small group or someone in your small group grow because of one of the resources? Write us at zpub@zondervan.com. We may read your message at a Zondervan employee meeting and together celebrate how God uses books to change people's lives.

Alicia Mey
Senior Marketing Director
Zondervan Book Group

THE COMPLETE BOOK OF QUESTIONS

Garry Poole

Everyone has a story to tell or an opinion to share. *The Complete Book of Questions* helps you get the conversational ball rolling. Created especially for seeker small groups, these questions can jumpstart any conversation. They invite people to open up about themselves and divulge their thoughts, and provide the spark for stimulating discussions. This generous compilation of questions can be used in just about any context to launch great conversations.

Questions cover ten thematic categories, from light and easy questions such as "What room in your house best reflects your personality?" to deeper, more spiritual questions such as, "If God decided to visit the planet right now, what do you think he would do?" *The Complete Book of Questions* is a resource that can help small group leaders draw participants out and couples, friends, and families get to know one another better.

Softcover: ISBN 0-310-24420-X

Pick up a copy at your favorite local bookstore today!

GRAND RAPIDS, MICHIGAN 49530 USA

WWW.ZONDERVAN.COM

BEGIN

BEGINNING
LIFE TOGETHER

life together
DOING

six sessions on
God's purposes
for your life

FOREWORD BY RICK WARREN

THE GOAL OF LIFE

By the time I finished college, I knew I wanted to live my life for Jesus Christ and nothing else. Nothing could compare to knowing and loving him. Todd had made the same commitment. This shared commitment seemed like the foundation for a happy marriage, so we took the plunge. It wasn't long, though, before reality rolled in like a tidal wave. We were mad at each other all the time! He had his way of doing things, and I had mine. Everything was a power struggle. We both loved Jesus and were even serving him full-time as our vocation. But there was one thing we'd overlooked: we had no idea how to love one another. We had built our house on a solid foundation, but the walls were flimsy and the roof was sagging.

Once this began to dawn on us, we set about learning to love. Day after day, year after year, we struggled but pressed on. We learned to put our own agendas aside, to believe in each other, to see each other as more important than ourselves. As I looked with new eyes at the extent of God's love for me, this understanding slowly transformed my heart toward Todd. Our marriage is still a work in progress, but God is teaching us how to build a house of love.

Learning to love has been a theme in all our relationships—with friends, coworkers, and even strangers. It's often easier to love God privately than to love the flawed people around us. But at the heart of God's purposes for us is his longing that we will learn to give and receive love as richly as he does.

—Denise

CONNECTING WITH GOD'S FAMILY   20 min.

Doing Life together begins with simply getting to know one another. A great way to do this is to tell something of your life story. In this session you'll begin on a lighthearted note by playing a game called "Two Truths and a Lie."

   1. The leader goes first. Tell the group three things about yourself. Two of these things must be true, and one must be something you've made up. Then each group member gets to guess

which of the three statements is false. After everyone has guessed, the leader reveals which statement was the lie. Each person who guessed right gets one point. The leader gets three points if no one guesses correctly.

Continue around the circle until everyone has told two truths and a lie. Then add up your points and give a round of applause to the winner.

2. It's important for every group to agree on a set of shared values. If your group doesn't already have an agreement (sometimes called a covenant), turn to page 61. Even if you've been together for some time and your values are clear, the Purpose-Driven Group Agreement can help your group achieve greater health and balance. We recommend that you especially consider rotating group leadership, setting up spiritual partners, and introducing purpose teams into the group. Simply go over the values and expectations listed in the agreement to be sure everyone in the group understands and accepts them. Make any necessary decisions about such issues as refreshments and child care.

GROWING TO BE LIKE CHRIST   30 min.

What's the point of life here on earth? Why does life together even matter? In a few brief sentences, Jesus sketches what's important in life:

> Hearing that Jesus had silenced the Sadducees, the Pharisees got together. [35]One of them, an expert in the law, tested him with this question: [36]"Teacher, which is the greatest commandment in the Law?"
> [37]Jesus replied: "'Love the Lord your God with all your heart and with all your soul and with all your mind.' [38]This is the first and greatest commandment. [39]And the second is like it: 'Love your neighbor as yourself.' [40]All the Law and the Prophets hang on these two commandments."
> —Matthew 22:34–40

3. Jesus says that loving God and loving our neighbors should be our two top life goals. Why do you suppose he chose these two goals instead of others? (For instance, why isn't self-fulfillment on his list? Why doesn't he cite a longer set of rules?)

4. *Love* is an abstract idea. On a practical level, how does a person go about loving God?

5. Share some examples of how people you know have loved a neighbor (family member, coworker, and the like) well. What does love look like in action?

6. Do you think it's possible to love God without loving our neighbors? Explain your reasoning.

7. What do you think happens when someone tries to love others without loving God?

Not long after this incident with the Pharisees, Jesus knew he was about to be arrested and killed. He gave his followers another command to add to the first two:

"*A new command I give you: Love one another. As I have loved you, so you must love one another. [35]By this all men will know that you are my disciples, if you love one another.*"
—John 13:34–35

8. How is this new command like the two earlier ones?

How is it different?

9. What's your reaction to the idea that the Christian life boils down to relationships—love for God and love for others?

10. In what situation this week will it be challenging for you to love God or others?

Loving God and others can't really be separated. Life together with God means life together with others, and vice versa. In the next five sessions of this study, you'll learn about five steps along a path toward learning to love God and others well. *Learning to love*—that's the point of life on earth.

SHARING YOUR LIFE MISSION EVERY DAY   10 min.

God is so full of love that he created humans so that he could love and be loved by us. He sent Jesus to draw us into his family of love. Love isn't meant to be hoarded; it's meant to be given away! You've now tasted a loving connection with each other in this group. The beginning of a group is a wonderful time to welcome a few new people into your circle.

11. Do you know anyone who would benefit from a group like this? Who could that person be? Think about family members, friends, neighbors, parents of your kids' friends, church members, coworkers, and the people who share your hobbies. Take a moment now to prayerfully list one or two names, and then share the names with your group.

_____   _____
            NAME   NAME

12. Pull an open chair into the circle of your group. This chair represents someone you could invite to join your group. Take a moment to pray together for the people whose names you wrote down.

Commit to

- making the call this week. Why not?—over 50 percent of those invited to a small group say yes! You may even want to invite him or her to ride with you.
- calling your church office to get the names of new members, and inviting new members who live near you to visit your group.
- serving your group by praying for and welcoming new people to your group.

 SURRENDERING YOUR LIFE FOR GOD'S PLEASURE 15–30 min.

13. Gather into circles of three or four people so that everyone has time to share and pray. Allow everyone to answer this question: "How can we pray for you this week?" You can write down prayer requests in the Prayer and Praise Report on page 74.

Take some time to pray for these requests. Ask God to empower you with love for the people on your hearts. Anyone who isn't used to praying aloud should feel free to offer prayers in silence. Or, if you're new to prayer and you're feeling brave, try praying just one sentence: "God, please help me to love _____."

STUDY NOTES

An expert in the Jewish law. The law is the teaching laid down in the first five books of the Bible—the very part of the Bible that Jesus quotes in this passage. The goal of life has been laid down from the beginning and hasn't changed.

Heart . . . soul . . . mind. These words overlapped in Jewish usage. The heart, for example, was regarded as the source of one's deepest beliefs, motives, desires, and feelings. It didn't signify merely the emotions. The point of using all these words was to emphasize the call to love God with *every* part of us—emotions, reasoning, imagination, passion, will, energy, and actions. Loving God is not just an emotion, nor is it just a belief. It also involves our will. We put our soul into it and do something to make love a reality.

Neighbor. The Jews debated who was and wasn't a "neighbor" who deserved love. Jesus expanded the word to include *everyone* who crosses our path (Luke 10:29–37). Today people who live on the other side of the planet are our neighbors, because our lives are linked with theirs.

☐ *For Further Study* on this topic, read Leviticus 19:9–18; Deuteronomy 6:4–5; 10:12–13; Proverbs 4:23; 1 John 3:16–18; 4:7–12, 20–21.

☐ *The Purpose-Driven Life Reading Plan:* Days 1–7

☐ *See page 73 for a checklist of the complete forty-day reading plan.*

Doing Life Together series

BRETT & DEE EASTMAN;
KAREN LEE-THORP;
DENISE & TODD WENDORFF

Based on the five biblical purposes that form the bedrock of Saddleback Church, Doing Life Together will help your group discover what God created you for and how you can turn this dream into an everyday reality. Experience the transformation firsthand as you begin Connecting, Growing, Developing, Sharing, and Surrendering your life together for him.

"Doing Life Together is a groundbreaking study ... [It's] the first small group curriculum built completely on the purpose-driven paradigm ... The greatest reason I'm excited about [it] is that I've seen the dramatic changes it produces in the lives of those who study it."

—FROM THE FOREWORD BY RICK WARREN

Small Group Ministry Consultation
Building a healthy, vibrant, and growing small group ministry is challenging. That's why Brett Eastman and a team of certified coaches are offering small group ministry consultation. Join pastors and church leaders from around the country to discover new ways to launch and lead a healthy small group ministry in your church. To find out more information please call 1-800-467-1977.

Curriculum Kit	ISBN: 0-310-25002-1
Beginning Life Together	ISBN: 0-310-24672-5 Softcover
	ISBN: 0-310-25004-8 DVD
Connecting with God's Family	ISBN: 0-310-24673-3 Softcover
	ISBN: 0-310-25005-6 DVD
Growing to Be Like Christ	ISBN: 0-310-24674-1 Softcover
	ISBN: 0-310-25006-4 DVD
Developing Your SHAPE to Serve Others	ISBN: 0-310-24675-X Softcover
	ISBN: 0-310-25007-2 DVD
Sharing Your Life Mission Every Day	ISBN: 0-310-24676-8 Softcover
	ISBN: 0-310-25008-0 DVD
Surrendering Your Life for God's Pleasure	ISBN: 0-310-24677-6 Softcover
	ISBN: 0-310-25009-9 DVD

GRAND RAPIDS, MICHIGAN 49530 USA

WWW.ZONDERVAN.COM

FULLY DEVOTED

living
each day
in Jesus'
name

JOHN ORTBERG
LAURIE PEDERSON
JUDSON POLING

WILLOW
CREEK
RESOURCES.

PURSUING SPIRITUAL TRANSFORMATION

What Is True Spirituality?

Reading by John Ortberg

L et's call him Hank. He had attended church since he was a boy, and now he was in his sixties. He was known by everyone—but no one really knew him. He had difficulty loving his wife. His children could not speak freely with him and felt no affection from him. He was not concerned for the poor, had little tolerance for those outside the church, and tended to judge harshly those who were inside.

One day an elder in the church asked him, "Hank, are you happy?"

Without smiling, he responded, "Yes."

"Well, then," replied the elder, "tell your face."

Hank's outside demeanor mirrored a deeper and much more tragic reality: *Hank was not changing.* He was not being transformed. But here's what is most remarkable: Nobody in the church was surprised by this. No one called an emergency meeting of the board of elders to consider this strange case of a person who wasn't changing. No one really expected Hank to change, so no one was surprised when it didn't happen.

There were *other* expectations in the church. People expected that Hank would attend services, would read the Bible, would affirm the right beliefs, would give money and do church work.

But people did not expect that day by day, month by month, decade by decade, Hank would be more transformed into the likeness of Jesus. People did not expect

No one really expected Hank to change, so no one was surprised when it didn't happen.

he would become a progressively more loving, joyful, winsome person. So they were not shocked when it did not happen.

How Is Spirituality Wrongly Understood?

How many people are radically and permanently repelled from The Way by Christians who are unfeeling, stiff, unapproachable, boringly lifeless, obsessive, and dissatisfied? Yet such Christians are everywhere, and what they are missing is the wholesome liveliness springing from a balanced vitality within the freedom of God's loving rule. ... "Spirituality" wrongly understood or pursued is a major source of human misery and rebellion against God.

—Dallas Willard, *The Spirit of the Disciplines*

Think of the irony: spiritual life leading to lifelessness. Spiritual growth producing misery. A life supposedly yielded to God rebelling against him! Obviously it's not supposed to be this way, yet for many, it's the sad truth.

When people are not being authentically transformed—when they are not becoming more loving, joyful, Christlike persons—they often settle for what might be called "pseudo-transformation."

We know that somehow we are supposed to be different than those outside the church. But if our heart isn't changing, we will look for more superficial and visible ways of demonstrating that we are "spiritual." We might:

- think spiritual maturity is simply about how much biblical or theological information we have acquired;
- think we should rigidly immerse ourselves in a host of spiritual practices or disciplines that will prove how spiritual we are;
- find ourselves looking down on people who are not working at their spiritual lives as hard as we are—so all of our efforts end up making us more judgmental and competitive rather than more loving; or

"Spirituality" wrongly understood or pursued is a major source of human misery and rebellion against God.

PURSUING SPIRITUAL TRANSFORMATION

- focus solely on outward behaviors, making them the litmus test of godliness, while ignoring deeper — and more destructive — sins of the heart.

We need only to hear Jesus' words to the religious leaders of his day to know that pseudo-spirituality is a deadly disease — and a common and contagious one at that.

What Is a Right Understanding of Spiritual Life?

When someone asks you, "How is your spiritual life going?" what comes to mind? How do you define spirituality? How do you assess spiritual progress?

Amidst all the confusing and distorted notions, Scripture speaks with brilliant clarity. "Whoever claims to live in him must walk as Jesus did" (1 John 2:6). To pursue spiritual life means simply this: *To know Jesus more intimately and to live as if he were in your place.* It is to order your life in such a way that you stay connected to Christ, thinking as he thought, speaking as he spoke, and walking as he walked.

To pursue spiritual life means simply this: To know Jesus more intimately and to live as if he were in your place.

Certainly, this imitation of Christ will look different for each person, expressing itself through that person's unique temperament, abilities, and circumstances. But there is a common denominator. At the core of Jesus' teaching is the command to love God with all your heart, soul, mind, and strength, and to love other people as you love yourself (Mark 12:30 – 31).

When someone asks you how your spiritual life is going, the real question is, "Are you becoming more loving toward God and people?" Regardless of anything else you measure, how you stand up against that statement will reveal your true spiritual stature. This measurement is the supreme spiritual diagnostic for Christ-followers who want to please him.

Doing Life in Jesus' Name

What would this kind of life look like if you actually lived it out? Let's face it — you could chalk up this concept as another idea that sounds good but isn't really practical. Yet God is inviting you to make each moment of every day a chance to learn from him how to master the art of life.

The apostle Paul put it like this: "Whatever you do, whether in word or deed, do it all in the name of the Lord Jesus" (Col.3:17). In the Bible, names often reflect a person's character. So to do something in Jesus' name means to do it in a way consistent with his character—to do it the way Jesus himself would.

Paul's teaching is very comprehensive on this matter. He says, "*Whatever* you do...." And in case anyone misses his point, he adds, "... whether in *word* or *deed*...." And in case anyone misses *that* he says, "... do it *all* in the name of the Lord Jesus" (italics added for emphasis).

God isn't interested in your spiritual life. God is simply interested in your life.

Your spiritual life is simply your whole life—every minute and detail of it—from God's perspective. In other words, God isn't interested in your spiritual life. God is simply interested in your *life*. And every moment is an opportunity to do life in Jesus' name.

One fully devoted follower, Brother Lawrence, put it this way:

> ... (W)hat makes you think that God is absent from the maintenance shop but present in the chapel? ... Holiness doesn't depend on changing our jobs, but in doing for God's sake what we have been used to doing for our own.
>
> Seriously—repair the equipment for God, answer the abusive phone calls for God, concentrate fully on the job you're doing for God. He isn't obsessed with religion—he's the God of the whole of life. But we need to give it to him, consciously turning it over into his hands. Then whatever we're doing—provided it is not against his will—becomes an act of Christian service.
>
> —David Winter, *Closer Than a Brother* (on the life of Brother Lawrence)

All of the everyday stuff of life can be filled with his presence—if you are. You *can* do what you're doing right now as Jesus would do it in your place. And if you do, you too will know the joy of true spiritual life.

Here is an experiment for putting Colossians 3:17 into practice. This week:

Memorize Paul's words in Colossians 3:17: "And whatever you do, whether in word or deed, do it all in the name of the Lord Jesus, giving thanks to God the Father through him."

Think about what it would mean for you to live the ordinary moments of your life as if Jesus were in your place. How would you do each of the following activities in Jesus' name?

- Waking up
- Greeting those you see first in the morning
- Eating
- Driving
- Working outside the home or caring for children while at home
- Shopping
- Watching TV
- Doing household tasks
- Reading the paper
- Going to sleep

Try it out. Focus on Jesus' presence with you as you go through the seemingly inconsequential moments of your day. Keep it simple; continually direct your thoughts back to him: ask for his help or his guidance, or simply share your heart with him.

Keep track of how the experiment goes. (If you don't already have a journal, we strongly recommend you start one so that you can keep a running list of observations throughout the duration of this study.) You will share your insights and experiences with the group when you meet.

1. Describe the picture Jesus paints in John 10:10 of what should happen in the life of all who follow him.

   What has prevented you or other Christians you know from having that quality of life?

2. Read Matthew 23:1−28. In this passage, Jesus has some harsh words for the religious leaders of his day. These scribes and Pharisees were well versed in Scripture and considered to be spiritually "in the know." If anyone understood what it meant to be spiritually mature, it was them—or so they (and those around them) thought. Yet Jesus was extremely frustrated by their spiritual shallowness and obsession with externals.

What specific behaviors does Jesus confront?

v. 3

v. 4

v. 5

NOTE: Phylacteries were little boxes with Scripture verses in them tied around the forehead—an obvious display of spiritual knowledge. The tassels on their garments were supposed to remind them to obey God (Num. 15:37–41), yet the Pharisees enlarged theirs to appear a bit superior.

vv. 6–7

v. 13

v. 15

vv. 23–24

NOTE: In those days, most everyone had little herb gardens. In an effort to be scrupulous, the teachers of the law and the Pharisees even gave a tenth of what those gardens produced. It would be like someone in our own day tithing on the dime they found on the street—not a bad thing, but petty in light of an utter failure to focus on more important aspects of justice, mercy, and faithfulness.

vv. 25–28

3. What heart attitude(s) do you think all these behaviors have in common?

4. As you read through this passage, was there any point at which you said, "Ouch—I have a tendency in that direction"? How do you think such distorted views of spirituality have crept into your life?

5. In your opinion, why is it easy for people to think that acquiring knowledge, following formulas, and obeying rules will automatically lead to true spiritual maturity?

6. According to the following words of Jesus, what must be at the heart of any concept of spirituality?

   Matthew 23:11–12

   Mark 12:28–34

   John 15:4–17 (hint: look for repeated words or phrases)

7. Being as candid as possible, how would you assess the state of your spiritual life right now?

What work would you invite God to do?

How can the members of your small group help?

TAKE-AWAY

My summary of the main point of this session, and how it impacts me personally:

NOTE: You will fill in this information after your group discussion. Leave it blank until the conclusion of your meeting.

continue the transformation . . .

29

A DISCUSSION GUIDE ON
HISTORY'S MOST IMPORTANT EVENT

Experiencing
THE
PASSION
of JESUS

LEE STROBEL / GARRY POOLE

WHO *REALLY* KILLED JESUS?

Every trial is a quest to determine who committed the crime in question. Is the defendant responsible, or is some other person really at fault? Jurors listen to testimony and examine exhibits—a process that's often dry, tedious, and complicated by dense legalese. It is not uncommon to see jurors nodding off during the seemingly interminable pauses and delays.

But what if the jurors could see a videotape of the crime itself? The drama and intensity would certainly captivate them. The images would be much more compelling than the words that would be used later to describe what had happened.

The Passion of the Christ illustrates the ability of film to engage its audience. In shock and disbelief, repelled by the brutality and suffering, we witness the gruesome crucifixion of Jesus—and our instinct for justice is stirred. "Who did this?" we want to shout. "Who's to blame for this atrocity?" The endless flogging, the swollen eye, the shredded flesh—all of the horrific violence compels us to demand, "Who is responsible? Surely the guilty party must pay for this!"

Is Satan behind it all? Judas? Pilate? The religious leaders? The Roman soldiers? The screaming mob? For that matter, why didn't the disciples step in and try to stop the madness? A lot of people were involved, and yet we can't seem to figure out who's primarily responsible.

Pilate orders the unjust execution, and Roman troops carry it out with inhumane efficiency. The disciples scatter, except for Peter, who denies Jesus in the midst of the confusion and chaos. The chants from the crowd create a terrifying rhythm in the background, jeering each step of Jesus' journey to Golgotha and every slam of the hammer. Judas, the betrayer, hangs himself. The sinister presence of a shrouded Satan is haunting. He—or is it she?—is eerily delighted when Jesus is finally pronounced dead.

In that swarm of characters and commotion, where do we point our finger of blame? Suspicion and sensitivity run high as we explore the list of potential perpetrators.

Of course, the depiction of Jesus' death has always created controversy, whether it is told through medieval passion plays or the latest filmmaker's interpretation. Amazingly, newspapers carried stories about the debate over *The Passion of the Christ* months before the film was even released. One concern was that the movie—even unintentionally—would focus blame on Jews collectively, vilifying them and encouraging anti-Semitism.

What is the truth behind the death of Jesus? Who are the real culprits? Our sense of justice requires a verdict. Maybe if we expose who is really to blame, we'll begin to make some sense out of the apparently senseless horror.

Open for Discussion

1. Name the movies you have seen that have dealt with the story of Jesus. Which one was the most powerful? Why?

2. What impact did *The Passion of the Christ* have on you? How did it inspire or surprise you?

3. What did you like most and least about the film? Which scene is most memorable for you?

4. Religious upbringing, the media, comments of friends, and even motion pictures can raise questions in our minds about Jesus. What questions or doubts are especially pressing to you?

In fact, if Christ himself stood in my way, I, like Nietzsche, would not hesitate to squish him like a worm.

CHE GUEVARA

5. Have you ever witnessed someone being treated unfairly and felt an intense desire for the perpetrator to be held accountable? Describe what happened.

6. How did *The Passion of the Christ* change your opinion about who was most responsible for Jesus' death? Who would you say the movie portrays as being guilty? Why?

7. What difference does it make who killed Jesus? How important is it to *you* to know who killed Jesus? Why?

8. How are the allegations concerning anti-Semitism supported or weakened by the fact that Jesus was Jewish, his closest friends and followers were all Jewish, he lived in a Jewish community, and he was hailed as a hero by Jewish crowds as he entered Jerusalem on Palm Sunday?

9. Take a few moments to read the verses below. Then, based on what those references suggest, complete the chart by listing the possible

I lay down my life—only to take it up again. No one takes it from me, but I lay it down of my own accord. I have authority to lay it down and authority to take it up again. This command I received from my Father.

JESUS CHRIST

accomplices to Jesus' death. How does your list clarify or confuse the issue for you?

Bible verses	Accomplices
Matthew 26:47–49	
Matthew 27:1	
Matthew 27:20–22	
Matthew 27:26	
Matthew 27:27–31	
Matthew 27:46	
Luke 22:3–4	
John 10:17–18	

10. Read the following Bible passages. Given the tension between God's sovereignty and human responsibility, who do you think the Bible claims is *ultimately* responsible for Jesus' death?

"Where do you come from?" [Pilate] asked Jesus, but Jesus gave him no answer. "Do you refuse to speak to me?" Pilate said. "Don't you realize I have power either to free you or to crucify you?"

Jesus answered, "You would have no power over me if it were not given to you from above."

John 19:9–11

[Jesus], being in very nature God, did not consider equality with God something to be grasped, but made himself nothing, taking the very nature of a servant, being made in human likeness. And being found in appearance as a man, he humbled himself and became obedient to death—even death on a cross!

Philippians 2:6–8

Do you think I cannot call on my Father, and he will at once put at my disposal more than twelve legions of angels? But how then would the Scriptures be fulfilled that say it must happen in this way?

JESUS CHRIST

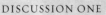

But God demonstrates his own love for us in this: While we were still sinners, Christ died for us.

Romans 5:8

He himself bore our sins in his body on the tree, so that we might die to sins and live for righteousness; by his wounds you have been healed.

1 Peter 2:24

My sins were the first to nail him to the cross.

MEL GIBSON

11. Do you agree with this statement made by Billy Graham after he saw *The Passion of the Christ*: "The film is faithful to the Bible's teaching that we are all responsible for Jesus' death, because we have all sinned. It is our sins that caused his death, not any particular group"? In what sense do you think we are responsible since we had not even been born when Jesus was crucified?

12. Check the statement(s) below that best describes your position at this point. Share your selection with the rest of the group and offer some reasons for your response.

_____ I'm not sure why the question of who killed Jesus is relevant.

_____ I'm convinced no single group of people alone is responsible for Jesus' death.

_____ I understand the Bible teaches we are all responsible for Jesus' death, but I'm not sure I believe it.

_____ I believe my sin and the sins of the world crucified Jesus.

_____ I believe the specific characters identified in the Bible each had a role in Jesus' death.

_____ I have all kinds of doubts about God, because it doesn't make sense to me that he would simply stand back and allow his son to be murdered without stepping in to stop it.

_____ I'm confused about how I could somehow be responsible for Jesus' death.

_____ Write your own phrase here: _____

_____

_____

> When you look at the reasons behind why Christ came, why he was crucified, he died and suffered for all mankind, so that, really, anybody who transgresses has to look at their own part in his death.
>
> MEL GIBSON

Scripture for Further Study

- Acts 2:22–24
- Romans 3:9–12, 21–26
- Romans 5:6–8
- 2 Corinthians 5:21
- Philippians 2:6–11
- 1 Peter 2:22–25

LOVE EACH OTHER

New Community
KNOWING. LOVING. SERVING. CELEBRATING.

Love each Other

1 John

SIX SESSIONS

WILLOW CREEK RESOURCES

JOHN ORTBERG
WITH KEVIN & SHERRY HARNEY

It's a Sin Thing

1 JOHN 1:5–2:2

Have you ever heard the phrase, "It's a God thing"? When something amazing happens, we exclaim, "It's a God thing!" When a prayer is answered in a clear and undeniable way, we declare, "It's a God thing!" When worship is invaded by the powerful and life-changing presence of the Spirit of God, we proclaim, "It's a God thing!" When a hardened sinner falls to his knees and surrenders to Christ, we agree, "It's a God thing!"

There is no other way to account for it! The fingerprints of God are all over these experiences, so we say, "It's a God thing!" Since hearing this phrase, I have willingly adopted it, because it expresses so much in so few words.

When we say this, there is no intention of being irreverent. We are simply saying God is real, active, and present right where we live. "It's a God thing" is a way to express what we have all experienced at one time or another. Our whole faith is built on the understanding that God works in human history. The ultimate "God thing" was the coming of Jesus Christ into the world and our lives.

But there is another phrase that needs to enter our language. It is not as much fun, but it is just as important. As a matter of fact, if we hope to say, "It's a God thing" often, we will need to first learn to say this other phrase. It has to do with our willingness to face up to the fact that there is darkness in us still. The phrase we must learn to speak is, "It's a sin thing!"

When we speak these words, "It's a sin thing!" we don't do so in accusation of others. Rather, it is a confessional statement all of us followers of Christ need to speak of ourselves. We take honest inventory, see our hearts and lives as they really are, and admit that the "sin thing" still has a grip on us. We need to admit that we still struggle with the lure, influence, and power of sin in our lives.

Making the Connection

1. What is one "God thing" you have experienced in the past year?

How have you seen the "sin thing" at work in your life?

Knowing and Being Known

Facing False Claims

In this first chapter, John identifies three false claims about sin. These claims always begin with the words, "If we claim ..." These deceptive claims were being lifted up by false teachers who were seeking to infect others with their erroneous understanding of sin. After identifying each false claim, John draws out some of the implications of this misunderstanding. Then John corrects the false teaching with the truth. He directs us to the correct teaching by using the key word *if*. Once we have the correct understanding before us, John draws out the reality of the powerful and life-changing implications of walking in the truth.

It is striking to notice that the false claims made by these deceptive teachers almost two thousand years ago still exist today. Not only are they being propagated by false teachers, but they lurk in the corners of each of our hearts. We need to shed light on these inaccurate views of sin and let the truth be known!

Read 1 John 1:5–7

2. John declares that God is light. What are some of the parallels we can draw between light and God?

3. What is the first claim the false teachers were making about sin (1:6)?

   What did John teach about sin to correct this faulty understanding (1:7)?

4. How have your relationships with others become more authentic since you have confessed your sins and become a follower of Christ?

Look in the Mirror

A prison of pride is filled with self-made men and women determined to pull themselves up by their own bootstraps even if they land on their own rear ends. It does not matter what they did or to whom they did it or where they will end up; it only matters that "I did it my way."

You've seen the prisoners. You've seen the alcoholic who won't admit his drinking problem. You've seen the woman who refuses to talk with anyone about her fears. You've seen the businessman who adamantly rejects help, even when his dreams are falling apart.

Perhaps to see such a prisoner all you have to do is look in the mirror.

—Max Lucado, *The Applause of Heaven* (Word, 1990)

Read I John 1:8–9

5. What is the second claim the false teachers were making about sin (1:8)?

What did John teach about sin to correct this false understanding (1:9)?

6. What are some of the traits and characteristics you see in the lives of people who are working overtime to prove to themselves, others, and God, that they are "good people" and not sinful?

How have you experienced freedom and peace when you have admitted your sinfulness to God?

7. John uses very strong words to describe those who have confessed their sins. He says we are *"purified* from *all* unrighteousness."* If you are a follower of Christ, describe the way that God sees you, in light of John's teaching.

Seeing Sin

The sins we see easiest in others we have learned first in ourselves; we know their behavior and their signs from the inside. Though they deny the personal fault, gossips spot gossips a mile away, as wolves know wolves by a familial scent. Is he neglectful? Impatient? Judgmental? Self-indulgent? Jealous? Scornful? Abusive? So, sometime and somewhere, were you—

Recall: that if you did not commit the sin against your spouse, yet you did, once, against your parents, your adolescent classmates, your friends, your colleagues at work, the teller in the bank, another race, another class of people, the poor. Or you did in your heart what you didn't have the temerity to do openly with your hands.

But recall these sins not to torment yourself, rather to rejoice in the forgiveness God has given you—you personally—since God was always at the other end of your sin, and did not return judgment for iniquity, but mercy.

—Walter Wangerin, Jr., *Measuring the Days* (HarperCollins, 1993)

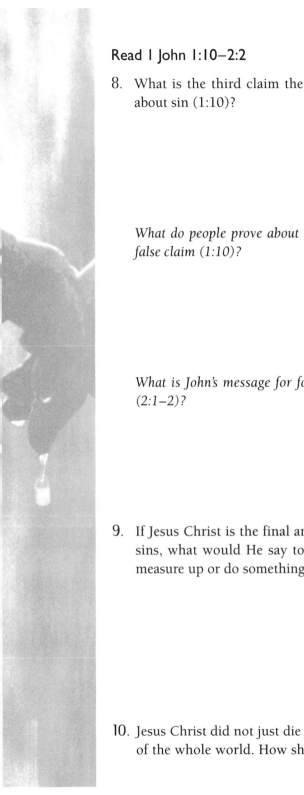

Read I John 1:10–2:2

8. What is the third claim the false teachers were making about sin (1:10)?

What do people prove about themselves if they accept this false claim (1:10)?

What is John's message for followers of Christ who do sin (2:1–2)?

9. If Jesus Christ is the final and complete sacrifice for our sins, what would He say to those who feel the need to measure up or do something to "pay for" their sins?

10. Jesus Christ did not just die for "my sins" but for the sins of the whole world. How should this truth influence the

way you will conduct yourself in the coming week in one
of the following places:

- In your workplace
- In your neighborhood
- In your shops or restaurants
- In your home

Celebrating and Being Celebrated

Take some time as a group to praise God for some of the "God
things" you have experienced in your own lives over the past
months. Let God know that you see His hand working and
that you celebrate His power at work.

Loving and Being Loved

Talk as a group about one member of your church who consistently communicates the love of Jesus to others. He or she
could be an up-front kind of leader, or a behind-the-scenes
person whom most people don't usually notice. Agree as a
group that each of you will drop this person a note or give him
or her a personal word of affirmation in the coming week.
Extend the love of Christ to this person who has been so faithfully walking in the light.

Serving and Being Served

Jesus did not just die for His followers. He died for all people: "He is the atoning sacrifice for our sins, and not only for ours but also for the sins of the whole world" (1 John 2:2).

If Jesus died for the world, and if God loves the world, we need to be willing to show His love through acts of service and charity. Talk as a group about one practical act of service you can extend to a person or family that does not yet know that Jesus died as the sacrifice for their sins. Contact this person or family and offer the service your group has agreed to extend.

Let your service connect with their life on three levels:

1. Bathe this experience in prayer. Pray that your loving service will show the love of God.
2. Bring your service with hearts filled with joy.
3. If those you serve ask why you have cared for them, let them know that your lives are overwhelmed by the love and grace of God and that you want to extend this to others.

New Community Series

BILL HYBELS AND JOHN ORTBERG WITH KEVIN AND SHERRY HARNEY

If you appreciate not having to choose between Bible study and building community, then you'll want to explore all eight New Community Bible study guides. Delve deeply into Scripture in a way that strengthens relationships. Challenging questions will encourage your group members to reflect not only on Scripture but also on the old idea of community done in a new, culturally relevant way.

Each guide contains six transforming sessions—filled with prayer, insight, intimacy, and action—to help your small group members line up their lives and relationships more closely with the Bible's model for the church.

Exodus: Journey Toward God	0-310-22771-2
Parables: Imagine Life God's Way	0-310-22881-6
Sermon on the Mount 1: Connect with God	0-310-22883-2
Sermon on the Mount 2: Connect with Others	0-310-22884-0
Acts: Rediscover Church	0-310-22770-4
Romans: Find Freedom	0-310-22765-8
Philippians: Run the Race	0-310-23314-3
Colossians: A Whole New You	0-310-22769-0
James: Live Wisely	0-310-22767-4
1 Peter: Stand Strong	0-310-22773-9
1 John: Love Each Other	0-310-22768-2
Revelation: Experience God's Power	0-310-22882-4

Look for New Community at your local
Christian Bookstore or by calling 800-727-3480.

WILLOW
Willow Creek Association

GRAND RAPIDS, MICHIGAN 49530 USA
WWW.ZONDERVAN.COM

REALITY
CHECK

SIX
DISCUSSIONS

Jesus'
secrets
Revealed

WINNING
AT LIFE

WILLOW
CREEK
RESOURCES

MARK ASHTON

ROLLOVER INVESTMENTS

ICEBREAKER

Think about the magazines you are likely to find in a grocery store line or a bookstore magazine rack. How do magazines like *Glamour, Sports Illustrated, GQ, Maxim,* or *Cosmopolitan* answer the question, "What is valuable?"

Justify your answers with articles, quotes, pictures, or ads.

Read Luke 12:22 – 34

Then Jesus said to his disciples: "Therefore I tell you, do not worry about your life, what you will eat; or about your body, what you will wear. Life is more than food, and the body more than clothes. Consider the ravens: They do not sow or reap, they have no storeroom or barn; yet God feeds them. And how much more valuable you are than birds! Who of you by worrying can add a single hour to his life? Since you cannot do this very little thing, why do you worry about the rest?

"Consider how the lilies grow. They do not labor or spin. Yet I tell you, not even Solomon in all his splendor was dressed like one of these. If that is how God clothes the grass of the field, which is here today, and tomorrow is thrown into the fire, how much more will he clothe you, O you of little faith! And do not set your heart on what you will *eat or drink; do not worry about it. For the pagan world runs after all such things, and your Father knows that you need them. But seek his kingdom, and these things will be given to you as well.*

"Do not be afraid, little flock, for your Father has been pleased to give you the kingdom. Sell your possessions and give to the poor. Provide purses for yourselves that will not wear out, a treasure in heaven that will not be exhausted, where no thief comes near and no moth destroys. For where your treasure is, there your heart will be also."

DISCUSS!

1. Jesus tells his followers not to worry about life's mundane needs. Look back at the things the magazines consider valuable. How could valuing these things cause worry?

2. Contrast the magazines' message with Jesus' message.

3. What is valuable according to Jesus' teaching—and do you think this is a realistic way to live?

4. In what ways are people similar to and different from the flowers and birds used as Jesus' examples?

5. From Jesus' words and your own experience, how do you imagine one might gain "treasure in heaven"?

Jesus' final statement, "for where your treasure is, there your heart will be also," is illustrated well in a story Jesus told to a greedy man.

Story (adapted from Luke 12)

Daniel Mulligan was an investing genius. In the mid '80s, he joined a tiny software firm that was about to hit it big. They paid him a decent salary with great stock options. By the time he cashed them in, Daniel was a multimillionaire. He continued working as an executive for the firm, carefully investing and growing his cash.

Sara Mulligan married Daniel just out of college. She stuck with him through years of seventy-hour workweeks and bore him two beautiful children — now 15 and 17. Daniel was a good provider, but wasn't home much. When he was, he spent most of his time on the computer, surfing sites like investwithme.com. Just like he was doing tonight.

By this time in their life and marriage, Sara didn't mind so much. She'd lived this way for years, and she was used to it. But tonight was different. Soon their life together would change. Over the years, Daniel had made enough money to allow them to live in luxury off the interest. Next month he would retire, and they could begin living the life they always wanted!

Sara and Daniel looked forward to traveling, reading, and spending time with the kids. "As soon as life slows down," they had always said, "we can care for the poor, visit our families, and do the significant thing we have always dreamed of." All their lives they had wanted to become more spiritual people, but the time at work never allowed for it. Next month would be different.

As usual, Sara went to bed while Daniel was still working on the computer. Like many other nights, she awoke about 3 A.M. with nobody at her side. Knowing she'd find her husband asleep at his desk, she slipped down the stairs to rouse him. Sure enough, she found him slumped over his computer . . . but tonight something was different. When she touched his shoulder, he was cold and his arm fell limp to his side. His skin was clammy, and he didn't awaken at her voice.

Above his lifeless body, the computer read "disconnected by invest-withme.com."

When the paramedic arrived, he told Sara that Daniel had died of a massive heart attack.

At his memorial service, people lauded his friendly demeanor, business savvy, and hard work ethic. But that night, at his gravesite, an angel of God had another adjective that best described him — expressed as he traced his finger over the tombstone, carefully and slowly tracing the letters F-O-O-L.*

DISCUSS!

6. What's the sobering point of this story?

7. What characteristics of Daniel or Sara do you recognize in people you know?

---

*Adapted from a message by John Ortberg, "It All Goes Back in the Box," given at Willow Creek Community Church, October 2000.

REALITY CHECK

Experts say that the best two indicators of your real priorities are your checkbook and appointment book or Palm Pilot. If someone else browsed your calendar and finances, what would they say your priorities are, and why?

One of Jesus' primary keys to winning at life is getting your priorities straight. How closely do your real priorities match up with what you want them to be? How well do they match up with God's priorities?

REALITY CHECK SERIES
by Mark Ashton

Winning at Life
Learn the secrets Jesus taught his disciples about winning at life through the stories he told.
Saddle Stitch
ISBN: 0-310-24525-7

Jesus' Greatest Moments
Uncover the facts and meaning of the provocative events of the final week of Jesus' life.
Saddle Stitch
ISBN: 0-310-24528-1

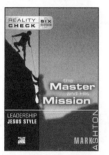

Leadership Jesus Style
Learn the leadership principles taught and lived by Jesus.
Saddle Stitch
ISBN: 0-310-24526-5

Hot Issues
Find out how Jesus addressed the challenges of racism, feminism, sexuality, materialism, poverty, and intolerance.
Saddle Stitch
ISBN: 0-310-24523-0

When Tragedy Strikes
Discover Jesus' perspective on the problem of suffering and evil in the world.
Saddle Stitch
ISBN: 0-310-24524-9

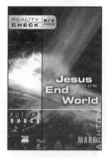

Future Shock
Uncover Jesus' perspective on the mysteries of the future as revealed in the Bible.
Saddle Stitch
ISBN: 0-310-24527-3

Sudden Impact
Discover the life-changing power of Jesus as he interacted with his contemporaries.
Saddle Stitch
ISBN: 0-310-24522-2

Clear Evidence
Weigh the arguments for and against the Jesus of the Bible.
Saddle Stitch
ISBN: 0-310-24746-2

www.zondervan.com/realitycheckcentral.org

ZONDERVAN™

GRAND RAPIDS, MICHIGAN 49530 USA

WWW.ZONDERVAN.COM

WILLOW CREEK

RESOURCES

www.willowcreek.com

"Push the pause button on whatever your small group is doing now and follow this guide—study it, discuss it, digest it, and apply it to your everyday life."

— Bill Hybels

THE
THREE
HABITS
OF HIGHLY
CONTAGIOUS
CHRISTIANS

A Discussion Guide for Small Groups

GARRY POOLE

foreword by Bill Hybels

HANG OUT TOGETHER

Building Relationships with Seekers

Jeff and I are next-door neighbors. When he and his family moved in about a year ago, my wife and I went over to welcome them to the neighborhood.

At first, that was the extent of our interaction since my time was limited and I really didn't want to add any more people to my already full life. I was very involved with the guys in my small group Bible study, I played in a church basketball league every Monday night with my four closest friends, and my wife and I socialized on a regular basis with the Christian couple across the street. Besides, it was obvious from the start that Jeff and I had different sets of values and morals. So I was reluctant to complicate my life with someone who was the polar opposite of everything I was or wanted to be and assumed our differences would make things awkward.

Unbelievably, that has all changed. One day, I decided to start praying for Jeff on a regular basis, and to my surprise, I found myself viewing him as someone who really matters to God—and to *me*. I began looking for ways to reach out and to get to know him better, and eventually got to the point where I started to genuinely care about the guy.

To top it off, I discovered that we had lots of things in common after all. We both follow sports pretty closely, so it was natural for us to get tickets to the Bears games at Soldier Field. When one of us needed help with a project around the house, the other was right there to pitch in. Now, whether it's a neighborhood block party, the Fourth of July, or just a picnic in the backyard, somehow we wind up together. We sincerely enjoy hanging out with each other, and I feel we have a pretty solid friendship. I can't get over how helpful Jeff has been to my family and me. When we're away on vacation or a business trip, he mows the lawn, grabs the mail, and checks on the house for us. And I can't count how many times this past winter I've come home late to find Jeff shoveling my driveway.

Early on in our friendship, Jeff confided in me that he was struggling in his job and was looking to make a change. Without hesitation, I gave Jeff a small clue about my relationship with God by letting him know I'd pray for him and his situation. When he ended up landing the job he'd been hoping for, he made a joke about my "special connection upstairs." That's when I gently inquired about any "connections" *he* had with God and confirmed that, although Jeff and his wife attend church from time to time, they probably were not Christians. We would, however, talk about spiritual issues occasionally, and I looked forward to those opportunities.

One such discussion went on late into the night after dinner at his house. Jeff's wife, Amy, concluded our dialogue with an amazing challenge. She said she'd recently wanted to get a Bible study started in our neighborhood, but hadn't felt that she or anyone she knew could lead it.

She wondered out loud if my wife and I would consider doing such a thing. "Maybe," I calmly replied as my heart pounded. I couldn't believe my own ears!

Yesterday, I was cutting the grass in my backyard when Jeff suddenly appeared out of nowhere and signaled me to cut the engine. He had just gotten off the phone with a cousin who had been hounding him to no end about Christianity. After declining an invitation to attend church for the umpteenth time, Jeff had received some "inside information" about me, his friendly neighbor! I wondered where in the world he was going with this. "My cousin told me you go to the same church he does," Jeff explained, "and since we're neighbors, he's hoping that maybe *you'll* be the one to finally convert me." *Thud.* I felt like crawling into a hole.

Jeff just stood there with eyebrows raised, waiting for my reaction. I frantically tried to smooth things over by explaining that I wasn't really trying to "convert" Jeff, but was simply open to talking with him about something that has come to mean so much to me. He turned to walk away, and I feared the worst. But then Jeff stopped and slowly turned with a smile.

"So, man ... am I your church project or your friend?"

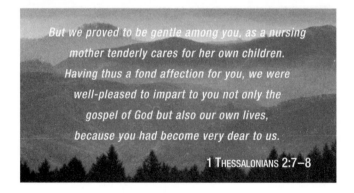

But we proved to be gentle among you, as a nursing mother tenderly cares for her own children. Having thus a fond affection for you, we were well-pleased to impart to you not only the gospel of God but also our own lives, because you had become very dear to us.

1 THESSALONIANS 2:7–8

Open for Discussion

1. Share the first name of a spiritual seeker (non-believer) you know fairly well. What is your relationship like? If you are unable to identify someone in your world who's seeking, what's something you could do to change that?

2. What motivates you to initiate and build friendships with seekers?

   What are the greatest obstacles that hinder the development of these friendships?

3. What fears and concerns do you suppose seekers might have about being friends with Christians? (Come up with as many of these fears and concerns as you can.)

4. Keeping the fears and concerns you just identified in mind, what might a seeker need from you to ensure that the relationship is going to be a safe one?

How would you rate your ability to create a safe context for such a relationship?

5. Read 1 Corinthians 9:19, 22–23. A basic ingredient to building meaningful relationships with seekers is a growing level of trust within those friendships. What can you do to build bridges of trust within the context of growing friendships with your seeking friends?

What could dismantle the bridges of trust between you and seekers?

Use the chart below to list the responses you and your group members come up with.

TRUST BUILDERS	TRUST BUSTERS

6. One of the most effective ways you can develop growing, authentic friendships with seekers is to identify areas of common interest, and then spend time together doing those things. For you and your seeking friends, what activities would those be? What specific steps will you take to initiate time together?

Heart Check

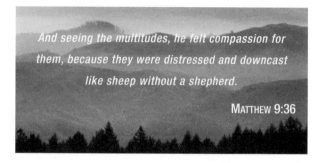

And seeing the multitudes, he felt compassion for them, because they were distressed and downcast like sheep without a shepherd.

MATTHEW 9:36

7. Read the Scripture in the box above. What did Jesus see when he looked at seekers?

How does Jesus' compassion impact you?

Is your response filled with feelings of motivation or guilt? Explain.

In what ways does your heart need to change in order for you to begin to see seekers through the eyes of Jesus?

8. Read 1 Thessalonians 2:7–8 in the box on page 17. It has been said that seekers don't care how much you know until they know how much you care. What are some ways you can authentically demonstrate your care for someone who is spiritually seeking?

9. Identify the two or three seekers you hope to see cross the line of faith someday. Use the Impact List on page 55 to remind you to pray for them on a regular basis.

Take some time now as a group to pray about your heart and attitude toward those seekers in your life, as well as your personal efforts to spend time with them.

Personal Profile

I first met Jay in middle school. As we began to hang out together, we would occasionally look each other straight in the eye and see both a friend and a competitor. We were in a lot of the same classes, where we would battle for the better grades. As it turned out, we both played trumpet in the band, and time after time we would shoot each other a grin before vying for the higher chair by playing a piece for the band director. "Jay, you're outta here," I'd say as I headed for the music room. And I'd beat him—only to be outdone by him the next time!

Most of all, we enjoyed competing in sports—baseball, wrestling, football—to list just a few. We thoroughly enjoyed this friendly kind of warfare; he'd slap me on the back as we entered the gym for a wrestling match and say, "Hey man, you're such a good friend, I'll almost feel bad when I pin you in ten seconds flat!" During our baseball games, if I picked up a bat and hit a home run, you'd better believe Jay would try his best to do the same. And if he snagged a fly ball with an impressive dive, I'd run all the harder to make an even more aggressive catch. Whatever the activity, we turned up the competitive heat.

But there was only one thing we didn't have in common—faith. I was a Christian; Jay, an atheist. By the time we were in high school, Jay was quite vocal about this major difference between us. And he didn't have any hesitation mentioning this fact to all who would listen. "God is just a figment of your imagination for your own convenience, to pacify you," he'd state. "There is no God. It's just something your parents talked about to scare you—and foolishly, you bought into it." It was almost like he was some kind of "atheistic evangelist."

Even in this area, our competitive natures emerged. As Jay eagerly explained his lack of belief in God, I openly told each others about the God I trusted and followed. We were equally confident about our own stance and demonstrated a strong conviction for what we believed. Yet, it was hard for me to fathom how someone with whom I had so much in common could feel so differently—exactly the opposite direction—about God.

One day, a group of us were on a road trip to a sporting event, and Jay decided to make things interesting. He had already gained a reputation for being an animated guy who enjoyed stirring up a crowd, so it didn't surprise any of us when he began to liven up our long bus ride through the flat farmland of northern Indiana.

He stood up in the front of the bus and yelled out a challenge. "Listen you guys. To make this ride more interesting, I think we should split up and have a big debate. So, whoever believes in God, sit on this side, and whoever doesn't believe God exists, sit on the other side." Curiosity—and an appreciation for Jay's courage and creativity—split us up just as he suggested. As we shifted from one side to the other, Jay continued. "I'll represent all the atheists, and Garry here will represent those of you who believe in God. Let's settle this once and for all!"

I went along with the idea and stood up next to Jay. Surprisingly, there were an equal number of kids on both sides of the aisle, and for the rest of the trip, that entire busload of students engaged in an exciting, intense discussion about the existence of God. I no longer remember all the specific arguments, but I do know that convictions ran deep and emotions were charged.

10. Read the personal profile above and identify the areas of common ground between Jay and the author as well as any hints that indicate that they really enjoyed their friendship.

11. Describe a seeker in your life with whom you have something in common and have the potential to spend time together. Dream out loud about what that scenario might look like to you. What's preventing you from taking steps to fulfill that dream?

Charting Your Journey

With this session, you're beginning a journey. And it could be the start of something thrilling as you learn to cultivate bridges of trust with your seeking friends. Just think about what God could do through you to reach the lost for him. So take full advantage of these sessions: ask the hard questions, think "outside the box," and learn from what others in your group have to say. Just be authentic about where you are in the process.

To help you apply what you're learning, the Charting Your Journey sections are designed to provide opportunities for you to indicate specific next steps in your process of reaching out to the seekers in your life. Don't be overly concerned if you are not yet where you want to be—it's a process. And this exercise is a step in the right direction. Progress takes time, but the important thing is for you to be open about where you are now and where you want to be in the near future.

12. Check any of the statements below that describe the specific next steps you would like to work on and apply in your life at this point. Share your selection with the rest of the group and give reasons for your response.

❑ I will prayerfully identify by name the seekers I hope to see cross the line of faith, and I will pray for them every day.

❑ Hanging out with seekers will become a higher priority in my life. I will arrange to spend time with a seeking friend this week.

❑ I will get more intentional about initiating activities with my seeking friends. I will block out some time to be with seekers each week over the next month.

❑ I really don't have any seeking friends in my life, and I'd like to change that. I will prayerfully initiate contact with a seeker and strive to form an authentic friendship with that person.

❑ My heart needs to be softened toward seekers. This month I will pray and study God's Word about developing a heart for the lost.

❑ I will identify and ask God to help me change the things I do that tend to drive seekers away from me.

❑ I will identify a need in the life of a seeking friend and reach out to meet that need this week.

❑ I will identify an area of common interest and regularly pursue that interest with my seeking friend.

❑ I want to see seekers through the eyes of Jesus. This week, as I see and interact with seekers in my world, I will pray for them and ask God to help me to see them as he does.

❑ Write your own phrase that describes a specific next step you will take in building relationships with seekers here:

Now go back through the above exercise and select the one action item you intend to implement first. Write that sentence in the space provided on page 57 of this guide.

Most of us can identify with the significance of the great commission, yet we struggle with where to start or how to stay motivated. Living out Jesus' call to share the life-giving good news is a big challenge, and sometimes, all we lack are some practical steps and tools to help us get going.

Welcome to *The Three Habits of Highly Contagious Christians!* You and your small group are about to embark on an exciting journey filled with possibility. The three sessions included in this guide have been specifically designed to sharpen your thinking about reaching out to seekers for Christ—and to ignite your heart to do it. Throughout each session, you will discuss practical ways to make a difference in the lives of people you know. Few things in life are as important as implementing the habits to become highly contagious.

Living an intentionally contagious Christian life really matters! It is, without a doubt, worth all the effort and risks involved. *The Three Habits of Highly Contagious Christians* will equip and inspire you to make an eternal impact through:

1. building relationships with seekers
2. sharing a verbal witness with seekers
3. bringing seekers to outreach events, services, and small groups

GARRY POOLE *is the director of evangelism at Willow Creek Community Church in South Barrington, Illinois. He is the coauthor of the best-selling Tough Questions series and author of* Seeker Small Groups *and* The Complete Book of Questions.

Cover design: Rob Monacelli
Cover photo: Terry Husebye / Getty Images

CHURCH AND MINISTRY / CHURCH LIFE / EVANGELISM & OUTREACH

US $7.99 / $12.99 CAN
ISBN 0-310-24496-X

ZONDERVAN™

WWW.ZONDERVAN.COM

WILLOW CREEK RESOURCES
www.willowcreek.org

TOUGH QUESTIONS

REVISED EDITION

"The profound insights and candor captured in these guides will sharpen your mind, soften your heart, and inspire you and the members of your group to find vital answers together."

— *Bill Hybels*

HOW DOES ANYONE KNOW GOD EXISTS?

HOW DOES

ANYONE

KNOW GOD

EXISTS?

WILLOW CREEK RESOURCES

GARRY POOLE

foreword by Lee Strobel

Is Anybody Out There?

In the Beginning — God?

Wouldn't it be great to know for sure about the existence of God?

For centuries, great minds—philosophers, theologians, and scientists—have argued various positions, hoping to settle the issue of whether or not God exists. Even today the topic is debated as intensely as ever. Sincere, intelligent people remain on all sides of the issue.

Why do some people seem so certain, while others remain skeptical? Where do you stand? If you believe he exists, how do you know? And if he doesn't, why are so many people convinced he does?

Most of us in this culture grew up hearing about God—as well as the Easter Bunny, Santa Claus, and the Tooth Fairy. Many of us said bedtime prayers. We hoped God would give us a new bike if we were good. Or we feared God's anger after stealing something from the drugstore.

Surrounded by such input since childhood, we have been ingrained with the idea of a "higher power." In fact, many people accept God as reality without even questioning. Yet as we get older, we outgrow childish dreams and fantasies. Once we learn the truth about the Easter Bunny, what do we do with God? Maybe he's the product of wishful thinking, too. Is there any evidence available for the existence of God? Or maybe

I didn't see any God out there.
—Yuri Gagarin, Soviet cosmonaut, after orbiting the earth

we shouldn't look for evidence—is God offended by people who need reasons for believing?

Often, people who have suffered greatly have the hardest time believing in God. Or at least they have trouble believing in the *goodness* of God. Norman Mailer, author of *The Gospel According to the Son*, shared this perspective: "If God is all good, then he is not all powerful. If God is all powerful, then he is not all good. I am a disbeliever in the omnipotence of God because of the Holocaust. But for thirty-five years or so, I have been believing that he is doing the best he can" (*Time*, May 5, 1997). Mailer is not an *atheist*, he's an *angry-theist*. The God of his childhood didn't fit into his adult world, so he had to redefine God— or abandon him.

What do *you* believe about the existence of God? How can you be sure? Is belief in God intellectual suicide? Tough questions . . . but worth taking the time to find answers. The purpose of these sessions is to guide you through a path of thoughtful contemplation about the existence of God and to invite you to explore and discuss all the options.

> The only reason that you hate to give up on the idea of "God" is simply because you've grown up and clung to the childhood fantasy that there's a "higher power."
>
> —Chuck, age 34, advertising copywriter

OPEN FOR DISCUSSION

1. Think back to your childhood. What did you believe about God during those years? Describe a few ways your views have changed since then.

2. What are some factors that have influenced your current beliefs about God?

STRAIGHT TALK

Positions About God

If you were to hit the streets, survey in hand, what do you think people would say about the existence of God? Certainly you would find a wide variety of answers. Here's a summary of the positions people take with respect to the existence of God:

- The *atheist* says no god or gods exist at all. "The universe happened by chance; there is no ultimate designer."
- The *agnostic* says it is not possible to know if there is a god or not. "God may exist, but no one can know for sure."
- The *deist* says God created the universe but has left it alone ever since. "God set the world in motion like a windup toy and does not get involved."
- The *theist* says God exists and is involved with creation. "God is not only out there, he cares about his creation and desires to have a continuing active participation in it."
- The *polytheist* says many gods exist. "You have a god, I have a god, and there are many gods out there."
- The *pantheist* says that God exists in and through everything in the universe and is one with the universe. "God is part of everything; he is in the trees, in me, in you — even in that survey you're carrying."

74

3. Which of the previous positions about God represents the most common belief among people you know? Which view is least popular among your friends and acquaintances? Give reasons for your answers.

> I contend that we are both atheists. I just believe in one fewer god than you do. When you understand why you dismiss all the other possible gods, you will understand why I dismiss yours.
>
> —Stephen Roberts

4. How convinced are your friends and acquaintances that their views and beliefs about God are accurate? What do you think determines the level of confidence they have?

5. How do you think most people decide what they're going to believe about God? On what do you think they base their beliefs about God?

> If God really does exist, I don't think he would have left it up to us to figure him out.
>
> —Tom, age 56, CEO

6. Which of the views of God listed makes the most sense to you? Why?

7. On a scale from one to ten (one represents low confidence and ten represents high confidence), how certain are you that your view is based on actual evidence rather than opinion?

8. What might help to increase the level of confidence you have in what you believe about God? Explain.

An atheist is a man who believes himself an accident.

—Francis Thompson

9. Frequently, we place our trust (that's what *faith* means) in people or things, even though we cannot know for sure they are trustworthy—such as when we board an airplane. What other specific examples can you give of "everyday faith"?

If there were no God, there would be no atheists.

—G. K. Chesterton

10. During those times when absolute proof is impossible (there is no guarantee a plane will arrive safely), what factors help you determine whether you'll place your trust in something?

All I have seen teaches me to trust the Creator for all I have not seen.

—Ralph Waldo Emerson

STRAIGHT TALK

Blind Faith

Belief in God does require faith, but it does not require blind faith. You do not have to toss reason and intelligence out the window to accept the existence of God. Concluding that God exists can be a reasonable faith decision.

11. Since it is possible to doubt anything—and therefore impossible to prove *absolutely* the existence of God (or anything else)—what factors would help you get to reasonable certainty concerning God's existence?

CHARTING YOUR JOURNEY

With this session you're beginning a journey. Keep in mind that you do not need to feel pressured to "say the right thing" at any point during these discussions. You're taking the time to do this work because you're looking for answers and because you're willing to be honest about your doubts and uncertainties. Others in your group would also benefit from hearing about what you'll be learning. So use these sessions profitably—ask the tough questions, think "outside the box," and learn from what others in your group have to say. But stay authentic about where you are in your journey.

To help you identify your progress more clearly, throughout this guide you will have opportunities to indicate where you are in your spiritual journey. As you gain more spiritual insights, you may find yourself reconsidering your opinions from session to session. The important thing is for you to be completely truthful about what you believe—or don't believe—right now.

12. Check the statement(s) below that best describes your position at this point. Share your selection with the rest of the group and give reasons for your response.

_____ There's nothing I can see that would change my opinion. I'm pretty sure there is no God—at least not the way Christians describe him.

_____ My beliefs may have been formed more by what others have taught me and not by what I really think.

_____ I think God exists, but I'm not sure I have solid reasons to back that up.

_____ I'm pretty sure God exists, but I don't know what impact that has on my life.

_____ Actually, this is an important topic. It's good to finally have a place to address questions like these.

_____ I believe God exists, and I'm hoping to learn more to understand him better.

_____ I believe God exists, but a personal opinion of this nature should be kept private.

_____ Write your own brief phrase here: _____

_____

_____

Scripture for Further Study

- Genesis 1
- Job 38–41
- Psalm 14:1
- Psalm 19
- Isaiah 40
- Acts 17:11–12
- Romans 1:18–32
- 1 John 1

TOUGH QUESTIONS

Garry Poole and Judson Poling

"The profound insights and candor captured in these guides will sharpen your mind, soften your heart, and inspire you and the members of your group to find vital answers together." —Bill Hybels

This second edition of Tough Questions, designed for use in any small group setting, is ideal for use in seeker small groups. Based on more than five years of field-tested feedback, extensive revisions make this best-selling series easier to use and more appealing than ever for both participants and group leaders.

Softcover

How Does Anyone Know God Exists?	ISBN 0-310-24502-8
What Difference Does Jesus Make?	ISBN 0-310-24503-6
How Reliable Is the Bible?	ISBN 0-310-24504-4
How Could God Allow Suffering and Evil?	ISBN 0-310-24505-2
Don't All Religions Lead to God?	ISBN 0-310-24506-0
Do Science and the Bible Conflict?	ISBN 0-310-24507-9
Why Become a Christian?	ISBN 0-310-24508-7
Leader's Guide	ISBN 0-310-24509-5

Pick up a copy at your favorite local bookstore today!

ZONDERVAN™

GRAND RAPIDS, MICHIGAN 49530 USA

WWW.ZONDERVAN.COM

six sessions

YOU & GOD . YOU & OTHERS . YOU & YOUR KIDS

mom

a mom's ordinary day

BIBLE STUDY SERIES

mothering without guilt

JEAN E.
SYSWERDA
general editor

written by
SHARON
HERSH

when guilt is good

> *Search me, O God, and know my heart;*
> *test me and know my anxious thoughts.*
> *See if there is any offensive way in me,*
> *and lead me in the way everlasting.*
>
> PSALM 139:23–24

 For You Alone

When you read the title of this study guide — *Mothering without Guilt* — did longing leap within your heart? Did you think, *"Oh, I want to mother without guilt,"* only to be quickly extinguished by another thought: *"But I feel guilty all the time."* Mothering without guilt is a reality many moms never experience because they can't distinguish between true guilt, which is good, and false guilt, which is a weapon of the enemy. The result? A nagging sense of guilt that becomes a constant and unwelcome companion.

Take a moment to examine your understanding of guilt and its role in your mothering by looking at the following statements. Check each one that applies to you.

Mothering without guilt means:

❑   There is a right way and a wrong way to do everything.

❑   I should never lose my temper with my children.

❑   I should spend at least an hour in prayer and Bible study daily.

❑   Everyone likes my children and me.

- ❑ We should always be on time.
- ❑ I should never be discouraged or grouchy.
- ❑ I should always be ready to correct my children when they make a mistake.
- ❑ I should check and double-check my work to make sure it is perfect.
- ❑ My children will never get sick if I am vigilant in taking care of them.
- ❑ I should anticipate problems before they occur.
- ❑ My children should get good grades in school.
- ❑ I can trust God to keep my children safe if I read my Bible every day.
- ❑ I should always make tasty, well-balanced meals that my kids love to eat!
- ❑ The house should be clean every night before I go to bed.
- ❑ My kids never talk back to me.
- ❑ My children always love to go to church.

If you checked any of these boxes, you probably have pockets of *false* guilt in your life and hopes of mothering without guilt seem pretty far-fetched. False guilt dupes you into believing the ideal is possible.

Look back at the list and underline how many times the words "should," "always," and "never" appear. False guilt nags at you with messages of "should" and "always" and "never." False guilt gains a foothold when other people in your life (especially your children) don't live the way you need them to live in order to satisfy your expectations.

Go back and look again at the boxes you checked. This time evaluate each one in light of these three questions:

- • Does achieving this goal require that you live perfectly with perfect children?

- • Does this goal allow for interruptions, mistakes, or individual personality traits?

- Is this goal dependent on your children conforming to your agenda?

Guilt is like quicksand. You can get stuck in it.

As long as you are tormented by false guilt, true guilt will be difficult to identify. True guilt is a blessing. Just as a pain in the body may be a warning of physical injury or sickness, guilt is an ache in the soul that signals you to examine your heart for sin. When you let go of the "shoulds" and stop evaluating your mothering by how well your children conform to your agenda, you have the opportunity to look beyond the false guilt to the true guilt pointing to sin that needs to be forgiven. You finally have the opportunity to see an *accurate* self-picture. That's when hope for mothering without guilt begins!

 ## For You and God's Word

Begin your study today by reading Psalm 139:23–24.

> Search me, O God, and know my heart;
>   test me and know my anxious thoughts.
> See if there is any offensive way in me,
>   and lead me in the way everlasting.

The psalmist David penned this intimate, open prayer. Whom do you trust with your every thought, motivation, choice, decision, or action? David laid his life open before God. He wanted God to see him and help him to accurately evaluate his pain and joy, weariness and vitality, selfishness and unselfishness, sin and service. Laying your life open before God makes it possible to move out of the house of fear and guilt into the house of love.

> Guilt can keep mothers narrowly focused on the question "What's wrong with me?" and prevents us from becoming effective agents of personal and social change.
>
> HARRIET LERNER, *THE MOTHER DANCE*

1. As you think about laying your life bare before God, what do you fear?

2. Do you believe that God can lovingly handle all that goes on in your mind and heart? Explain your answer.

When you don't believe God can be trusted, you become defensive, deny your harmful or hurtful ways, and deflect any hope of change. When you believe that God loves you and longs to forgive you and have an intimate relationship with you, you can look courageously at your life and change can become possible.

Honestly ask yourself, "Do I want to defend myself, or am I willing to open my heart to God's gaze?" "Do I want to deny any hurt or harm I may have caused, or will I allow God to evaluate my actions, reveal their consequences, and offer forgiveness?" "Do I blame others or the circumstances, or can I ask God to unveil my responsibility?"

Your ability to examine yourself accurately is wholly dependent on what you believe about God's love and forgiveness.

3. Recall a time when your young child made a foolish or willful mistake. What did you feel for your child?

> *Never was a mother so blind to the faults of her child as our Lord is toward ours.*
>
> DANIEL CONSIDINE, *CONFIDENCE IN GOD*

Do you believe God to be distant, easily annoyed, indifferent, or angry? Is he always watching you so that he can catch you in your sin and punish you? Do you believe that God is harsher with you than you are with your own child? Pray the words of Psalm 139:23–24, focusing on a God who is completely loving and completely trustworthy. Can you bare your heart before him? Can you be honest? Now write out the prayer of Psalm 139 in your own words, and use it throughout the week in your prayer times.

 ## For You and Others

Begin your time together as a small group by discussing this question: *What is the deepest need of the human heart?*

Look back at the boxes you checked in "For You Alone." What do these statements suggest that you may *think* is your greatest need?

1. Look up each of the following Bible passages, discussing what each one says about your deepest needs:

Mark 2:5, 9 _____

Luke 7:47–48 _____

Colossians 2:13 _____

Do you agree that this is your deepest need? Why, or why not?

2. Recall a time when one of your children asked for forgiveness. What did you feel for your child?

What could your feelings toward your child tell you about God's feelings toward you when you need forgiveness?

3. Describe an experience of forgiveness that has been life-changing for you or for someone you know personally.

Read Psalm 139 together. Have each person in your study read out loud a verse from this psalm, then discuss the following questions:

4. What does Psalm 139 suggest God knows about you? Be specific.

How does this intimate knowledge make you feel?

5. Discuss how the "shoulds" in your life (see the list in "For You Alone") can get in the way of trusting God with an intimate knowledge of who you really are.

6. What is your understanding of intimacy with God? What does it mean in day-to-day living?

7. Do you believe that greater intimacy with Jesus is the only antidote for guilt? If yes, state why. If no, state what could also be an effective antidote for guilt.

8. David, the man after God's own heart (Acts 13:22), was no stranger to failure, shame, disappointment, and sin. Yet he wasn't afraid to have God "search," "know," "test," and "see" him. Check out these verses, noting what David is confident of in each one:

Psalm 13:5 _____

Psalm 18:19 _____

Psalm 26:3 _____

Psalm 27:13 _____

Psalm 52:8–9 _____

Psalm 56:3–4 _____

 ## For You and God

Once you cast off false guilt and trust God to search you, know you, test you, and see you in his perfect love, you can stop struggling and relax. Seeing yourself as God sees you will result in less shame and fear. The apostle John wrote, "There is no room in love for fear. Well-formed love banishes fear" (1 John 4:18 THE MESSAGE).

Find a quiet place. While there, confess your trust in God's love, and ask him to gently reveal and help you banish any false guilt. Then ask him to uncover any remaining ache in your soul — any true guilt. Here are two exercises that can help you lay yourself bare before God:

- Take out a piece of paper and write down everything you are holding against yourself in your mothering. Include past failures as well as current struggles. Be as specific as possible. Offer them to God for his forgiveness, and then either burn your list or tear it into tiny pieces, knowing that "He forgives your sins — every one" (Psalm 103:3 THE MESSAGE).

- Write about a shame-filled moment as a mother — yelling at your child, neglecting your child's needs, disregarding your child's feelings, being overcome by personal temptations and struggles, and so forth. Describe in detail every smell, sight, sound, and touch of this moment. Invite God into your story, asking for a sense of the fullness of his unconditional love and forgiveness. Then burn or tear up that piece of paper as a symbol of God's complete forgiveness.

 ## For You and Your Kids

One of the wonderful by-products of intimacy with God is that you will be able to live humbly and authentically before your children, modeling to them the liberation of forgiveness. A study done several years ago reveals that the most influential interactions between parent and child are those where parents seek forgiveness from their children for their wrongdoings. Children who experience their parents asking for forgiveness develop confidence that they can take risks, make mistakes, and remain secure in relationships (see the book *Parenting by Heart* by Ron Taffel, with Melinda Blau [New York: Addison-Wesley, 1991]).

Preschool–Elementary

Do you remember pretending to be a mommy when you were a little girl? When your child pretends to be a mommy or a daddy, talk with her or him about the qualities of a parent that this pretend play reveals. Does their play or your conversation uncover ways in which you have failed your child? Take time to ask for forgiveness and to talk about ways you can better mother your children.

Middle–High School

Look together at the messages of your culture (magazines, movies, and advertisements)—what these messages say are your greatest needs. What does your culture suggest you need most? Wear certain brands? Have the right look? Acquire more stuff? Share with your children some of your own misconceptions about your deepest needs. Look for opportunities to remind your children that the deepest need of the human heart is to be fully known and forgiven by God.

All Ages

The message of God's story is that forgiveness is always available—you just have to ask. How can you translate God's message to your children? As you live in the fullness of God's forgiveness of your sin, you will be able to offer forgiveness to your children and at the same time point them to God. Don't miss the incredible opportunity that arises in the midst of failure—the opportunity of forgiveness. When you know you are forgiven—completely known and completely forgiven—you can mother without guilt.

> *Forgiveness is an answer, the divine answer, to the question implied in our existence. An answer is an answer only for him who has asked, who is aware of the question.*
>
> PAUL TILLICH,
> "TO WHOM MUCH WAS FORGIVEN"

A Mom's Ordinary Day

Jean E. Syswerda, General Editor

The eight Bible studies in this series are designed specifically to help a mom find wisdom from God's Word as she seeks to be the best mom, person, and disciple she can be.

Each study contains six sessions divided into five flexible portions: For You Alone, For You and God's Word, For You and Others, For You and God, and For You and Your Kids. The last section helps moms share each week's nugget of truth with their children.

<u>Softcover</u>
Finding Joy in All You Are 0-310-24712-8
Gaining and Being a Friend 0-310-24713-6
Growing Strong with God 0-310-24714-4
Mothering without Guilt 0-310-24715-2

Making Praise a Priority 0-310-24716-0
Managing Your Time 0-310-24717-9
Entering God's Presence 0-310-24718-7
Winning over Worry 0-310-24719-5

Pick up a copy at your favorite bookstore!

ZONDERVAN™

GRAND RAPIDS, MICHIGAN 49530 USA

WWW.ZONDERVAN.COM

WOMEN OF FAITH®

BIBLE STUDY SERIES

Becoming a Woman God Can Use

A Study on Esther

Judith Couchman

Foreword by Thelma Wells

Who's in Control?

When life feels out of whack,
God is still working.

Vashti smiled at the ornately dressed noblewoman seated next to her and asked, "So, what have you thought of the king's grand party?"

"Magnificent!" the woman exclaimed. "My husband says it has boosted his confidence in King Xerxes and his ability to conquer the Greeks in battle."

"Ah, yes, the Greeks. I almost forgot about them," sighed Vashti.

The noblewoman laughed, but Vashti did not. For half a year her husband had presided over a massive celebration for their kingdom, with princes and paupers traipsing through the palace day and night. Xerxes had explained that before waging war, he wanted to exhibit wealth and strength to his subjects and the world. "It will make our warriors proud and our enemies afraid," he'd said, crossing his arms with satisfaction. But Vashti knew that even without the pending conflict, Xerxes delighted in showing off his power and possessions—and he loved to eat, drink, and be merry.

And that six months was enough to make any wife weary.

Tonight, during the celebration's final banquet, Vashti had distanced herself from the king and his drunken men by entertaining visiting women in the palace. It was a workable feast for her, until halfway through the meal the king's attendants materialized at the banquet door.

"The king commands that you appear at his feast, wearing your royal crown," they announced. Their words murmured through the banquet hall and hushed the queen's chattering guests.

"Why? Why does he need me?" insisted Vashti, but she knew the answer. She was to display herself to the king's rowdy guests.

Deborah ate a few bites of the cake of ground dates she'd made the day before and broke off a piece to take with her. She was ready to begin the day's work.

The moment she walked outside, she caught the morning sky's splendor. The colors! Mauve, peach, almost yellow. She felt a sudden awe, a hush, and bowed her head to whisper words of praise. Calmed now and joyful, she began climbing the hill toward the palm tree. Clusters of golden dates hung from it like huge bells. Underneath this palm tree, she listened to her people's grievances and judged their cases according to Jehovah's laws.

When Deborah reached the top of the hill, she settled under the tree and waited. Soon she spotted a small group of people on the road below. Voices traveled on the wind, loud and sharp. Two men gestured angrily as they climbed the hill. A woman and child walked behind them holding hands.

"Please, Lord," prayed Deborah. "Give me wisdom."

Setting the Stage

WHAT DOES DIFFERENT MEAN?

In the next weeks your group will study Deborah, a woman who dared to be different. Different from the "normal role" for women in her culture; different in values from the pagan beliefs surrounding her; different in the way she handled her success. But the most important difference was that she committed her life to God. Deborah was different not for herself, but for him.

How does someone become different — and make a difference — for God? Author and theologian C. S. Lewis explained it this way:

> The Christian way is different: harder, and easier. Christ says, "Give me All. I don't want so much of your time and so much of your money and so much of your work: I want You. I have not come to torment your natural self, but to kill it. No half-measures are any good. I don't want to cut off a branch here and a branch there, I want to have the whole tree down. Hand over the whole natural self, all the desires which you think innocent as well as the ones you think wicked — the whole outfit. I will give you a

new self instead. In fact, I will give you Myself; my own will shall become yours."

Before attending the first group session, think about what "being different for God" means to you. Jot down your thoughts about these questions:

- To you, what does it mean to be different for God in your daily life?

- How do you feel about C. S. Lewis's definition of the "Christian way" being different? What would be hard about it? What would be easy?

- If you dared to be different for God, how might your life change?

- How would you like to make a difference for him?

Close this time with an honest prayer to God about how you feel about being different for him.

SESSION ONE – *One of a Kind*

Discussing Deborah's Story

THE FIRST AND ONLY

Deborah was the first and only female judge in ancient Israel. That's quite an accomplishment by itself. Judges led the people, interpreted national laws, and commanded military forces. But Deborah also was fair, trustworthy, and God-fearing. These were hard-to-find attributes during the chaotic times recorded in the Old Testament book of Judges. Still, Deborah held firm, and dared to be different for God.

Before you begin the discussion, read the Bible text, Judges 4:1–5.

1. In verses 1–2, read about Israel's plight after the judge Ehud died. What kind of new leader did Israel need?

2. During this time, what roles did Deborah serve in her personal and professional life? See verses 4–5.

3. Read the Behind the Scenes section, "The Role of Judges," on page 24. What characteristics did Deborah need to be an effective and honorable judge of Israel?

4. What challenges did Deborah face leading the Israelites during this era?

5. As a judge, Deborah fulfilled an unusual position for a woman in her culture. How might she have garnered such universal respect from her people? Consider at least three possibilities.

Sharing Your Story

TAKING THE DARE

Even though Deborah lived thousands of years ago, her difficulties and victories represent the path of women who pursue God and his will. No matter the era, no matter the calling, the Lord asks us to "come out from them and be separate" (2 Corinthians 6:17). When we do, it's a distinctive journey.

1. Reread the Setting the Stage section "What Does Different Mean?" on pages 20–21, through the quote by C. S. Lewis. As a group, complete this sentence, writing it on a whiteboard or easel pad so everyone can see it. "Being different for God means . . ."

Behind the Scenes

THE ROLE OF JUDGES

Judges were military heroes or deliverers who led the nation of Israel against their enemies during the period between the death of Joshua and the establishment of kingship. The stories of their exploits are found in the book of Judges.

During the period of the judges, from about 1380–1050 B.C., the government of Israel was a loose confederation of tribes gathered about their central shrine, the ark of the covenant. Without a human king to guide them, the people tended to rebel and fall into worship of false gods time and time again. "Everyone did what was right in his own eyes" (Judges 17:6; 21:25) is how the book of Judges describes these chaotic times. To punish the people, God himself would send foreign nations or tribes to oppress the Israelites.

These judges or charismatic leaders would rally the people to defeat the enemy. As God's agents for justice and deliverance, they would act decisively to free the nation from oppression. But the judges themselves were often weak, and their work was short-lived. The people would enter another state of rebellion and idolatry, only to see the cycle of oppression and deliverance repeated all over again.

The judges themselves were a diverse lot. Some of them received only a brief mention in the book of Judges.... The careers of the other judges are explored in greater detail in the book of Judges. Othniel, a nephew of Caleb (3:7–11), was a warrior-deliverer who led the Israelites against the king of Mesopotamia. Ehud (3:12–30) was distinguished by left-handedness and his deftness with a dagger. Jephthah (11:1–12:7) was a harlot's son whose devotion to God was matched only by his rashness. Gideon (6:11–8:35) needed many encouragements to act upon God's call. But he finally led 300 Israelites to defeat the entire army of the Midianites. The most interesting of the judges, perhaps, was Samson (13:1–16:31), whose frailties of the flesh led to his capture by the hated Philistines. The most courageous of the judges was Deborah, a woman who prevailed upon Barak to attack the mighty army of the Canaanites (4:1–5:31).

The stories of the judges make interesting reading because of their rugged personalities and the nature of the times in which they lived. The openness with which they are portrayed in all their weaknesses is one mark of the integrity of the Bible.

— Ronald F. Youngblood,
Nelson's New Illustrated Bible Dictionary

2. How can you distinguish between "being different for God" and being rebellious? For example, if you decide to "go against the crowd," how do you know whether you're following God's desire or your own?

3. In our culture, what challenges face a woman who dares to be different for God? How can you overcome these challenges? Write both lists on a whiteboard or easel pad.

4. What could be the benefits of being different for God? Divide into pairs and discuss this question. Then share your answers with the whole group, listing them on the board or easel pad. As a group, choose the top three benefits of being different for God.

In the next weeks you'll discover that for Deborah, following Jehovah was challenging and surprising, exciting and satisfying. God wants the same for you. So get ready. Take the dare. Become different for God.

Prayer Matters

LORD, I AM THINE

Finish today's session with a group prayer of dedication to God, expressing your desire to follow him. Begin by reading aloud in unison this prayer from a Methodist covenant service. Then each woman can add a short statement about how she desires to be different for God. Your leader can close with a brief prayer.

> *Dear Lord,*
> *I am no longer my own, but thine.*
> *Put me to what thou wilt, rank me with whom thou wilt:*
> *Put me to doing: put me to suffering:*
> *Let me be employed for thee, or laid aside for thee:*
> *Exalted for thee, or brought low for thee:*
> *Let me be full, let me be empty:*
> *Let me have all things: let me have nothing:*
> *I freely and heartily yield all things to thy pleasure and disposal.*
> *And now, O glorious and blessed God, Father, Son, and Holy Spirit,*
> *Thou art mine and I am thine. So be it.*
> *Amen.*

DISTINCTLY DIFFERENT

God has already made you distinctly different from anyone else. This week, consider how this uniqueness can accomplish God's will for you and the world you live in.

With a friend: Plan to do something fun and "distinctly different for God" together. Something that detours from your usual routine and expresses God's love to the world. Take cookies to teachers at your child's school, offer to shape up an elderly person's yard, or volunteer at a nursing home. Or be unusual and offer to buy a stranger's meal at a fast-food restaurant or pool together and pay for a financially struggling person's utility bill. Be thoughtful and creative!

On your own: During your private time with God, pull out a piece of paper and a pencil. Place your palm on the paper, spread out your fingers, and trace around the hand with the pencil. On each outlined finger, write a talent or attribute that characterizes you.

Pray and ask God how you could use each characteristic for him. Then at the tip of each finger, write a few words that describe how you might use the corresponding trait to be different for God. For example, you could write "compassionate" on a finger and "invite homeless people for dinner" at the tip of it.

Keep the drawing in your Bible or journal. Choose one characteristic to begin with, but also prayerfully plan how to use all five traits for God.

Words to Remember

YOUR LIFE, GOD'S WILL

> Teach me to do your will,
>
> for you are my God;
>
> may your good Spirit
>
> lead me on level ground.
>
> — Psalm 143:10

Women of the Bible
Judith Couchman, Janet Kobobel Grant

Through intriguing stories of biblical women, the Women of the Bible study series helps readers see how God wants to work in their lives. Questions and activities are designed to encourage personal application, understanding, and prayer, and to foster interaction within study groups.

Becoming a Woman God Can Use: A Study on Esther: 0-310-24782-9
Choosing the Joy of Obedience: A Study on Mary: 0-310-24784-5
Daring To Be Different: A Study on Deborah: 0-310-24781-0
Entrusting Your Dreams to God: A Study on Hannah: 0-310-24783-7
Facing Life's Uncertainties: A Study on Sarah: 0-310-24786-1
Trusting That God Will Provide: A Study on Ruth0-310-24785-3

Pick up a copy today at your favorite bookstore!

ZONDERVAN™

GRAND RAPIDS, MICHIGAN 49530 USA

WWW.ZONDERVAN.COM

WOMEN OF FAITH℠

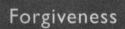

Forgiveness

WOMEN OF FAITH™
BIBLE STUDY SERIES

Embracing
Forgiveness

Foreword by
LUCI SWINDOLL

Forgive and Forget?

W e've all heard the horror stories about hurting people who've been given advice by well-meaning but gravely misguided believers.

- "I understand that he hit you last night, but God says you are to turn the other cheek and submit to your husband."
- "Yes, you were abused, but that was twenty years ago. Get over it! Besides, he *is* your father, and the Bible says we're supposed to honor our parents."
- "Forgiveness is simply a decision made in obedience to Jesus' command. Just do it. If her offense still bothers you after that, then you must not have been sincere."
- "If you've really forgiven her, then you'll forget what she did and carry on the relationship as before. It doesn't matter whether or not she's sorry; the Bible says you are to love her and forgive her seventy times seven!"

Perhaps you've gotten some similar direction yourself—or you've given it in your earnest desire to offer biblical counsel. As believers we want to imitate God, as Scripture commands (Eph. 5:1). We know we are to love one another as he has loved us, so sometimes we harness ourselves to the heaviest yoke within reach and trudge forward in our valiant attempt to obey his toughest commandments.

But is that what he expects? Then what did he mean when he told us to come to him for rest because his yoke is easy and his burden is light

(Matt. 11:28–30)? Perhaps we make his commands to love and forgive more rigorous than he meant them to be. Perhaps in our sincere desire to please him, we've perverted part of his intent.

In this lesson we'll explore what biblical forgiveness is and what it is not. You may find that you've been pulling a load you need to leave on God's shoulders.

> *Love is the power behind forgiveness. But it*
> *does not work the way a lot of people suppose. Love is not*
> *a soft and fuzzy sentiment that lets people get away*
> *with almost everything, no matter what they do to us.*
> *Love forgives, but only because love is powerful.*
> LEWIS B. SMEDES

A Moment
for Quiet Reflection

1. Make room for at least fifteen minutes of private time and settle in to ask yourself some questions. What do you think forgiveness is? How does it look? Reflect on your personal definitions and write them down.

2. In what specific ways has your perspective on what it means to forgive been influenced by what your family or religion has taught you?

3. Do you see these influences as positive or negative or both? Why?

Knowing God's Heart

1. As a group, discuss what you feel and believe about the following common conceptions of forgiveness. Do you agree with them or not? Why?

   - Forgiveness means forgetting about the offense.

   - Forgiveness involves excusing the offender.

   - Forgiveness requires giving up the desire for vengeance.

   - Forgiveness is about freeing oneself from the past.

   - Forgiveness means "letting bygones be bygones."

   - Forgiveness requires accepting the offender just as he is.

   - Forgiveness results in reconciliation of a broken relationship.

2. Are any of the definitions from Question 1 on the list you made in "A Moment for Quiet Reflection"? Share with the group some of your personal conceptions that are the same or different.

3. Besides Jesus himself, few people in Scripture teach us more about forgiveness than Joseph does. One of two sons born to Jacob and Rachel, Joseph was the envy of his brothers, the other eleven sons of Jacob. Joseph was Jacob's favorite, and a bit spoiled and full of himself, so out of jealousy and spite his brothers sold him to some merchants they met along a road. "He's been killed by wild beasts," they lied to their father—(*and good riddance*, they thought). Little did they know that their little brother was sold again, this time to an Egyptian official named Potiphar.

God's favor was on Joseph, a handsome and intelligent seventeen-year-old, and in no time he was put in charge of everything Potiphar owned. After Potiphar's wife double-crossed Joseph, he spent over a decade in prison. But through a series of divine events the young Hebrew slave got the favorable attention of Pharaoh and eventually became the ruler of all of Egypt.

Enter Joseph's brothers stage left. Hoping to avoid starvation during the famine at home, the ten oldest trekked to Egypt to buy food from the guy in charge. Joseph recognized them instantly, but they didn't know him. After testing their character through a few tricky schemes, Joseph revealed his identity.

Read Genesis 45:1–15 aloud together. When Joseph came clean, how did his brothers respond? Why?

4. Compare Joseph's actions in verses 3 and 4. What is significant about the way he relates to his brothers in verse 4?

5. Joseph feels and expresses a great deal of emotion right
before he reveals his identity. What does this intensity suggest about the consequences of withholding forgiveness
and the probable results of finally extending it?

6. In verse 4 we are given one more key insight into the
nature of forgiveness. What do the last five words of this
verse imply?

7. In spite of the fact that Joseph had suffered and had spent a good part of his life in captivity because of his brothers' actions, he looked at his entire experience in a positive light. What do verses 5–8 suggest about how he did this? (Also take a moment to read Genesis 50:19–21, which reaffirms Joseph's perspective.)

8. Because of his perspective on his suffering, Joseph was able to let his cruel brothers "off the hook." What do you think is the specific lesson here about the nature of forgiveness?

9. Joseph not only reassured his brothers of his goodwill, but he invited them to bring all their relatives and flocks to live in Egypt at his expense so they would not starve during the famine. Before sending them back to Canaan to fetch his father, Jacob, and all their stuff, Joseph demonstrated his complete forgiveness once more by embracing and kissing the men who had once shown no regard whatsoever for his life. What do verses 14 and 15 suggest about how a fully reconciled relationship might look and feel?

10. It is critical to understand that the reconciliation between the victim and perpetrators in this story did not come as easily as these few verses might suggest. Before Joseph revealed his identity and welcomed his brothers back into his life, he put them through the paces to discern just who he was dealing with. Had the boys who sold him off for a few pieces of silver become men whose hearts were just as dark? Or had his brothers changed? Would they be capable of engaging in a "safe" relationship with him in the future? During your own Bible reading time in the week ahead, you might want to read the entire account in Genesis 42–44 of how Joseph tested his brothers. For now, what do you think Genesis 44:33–34 indicates about the heart of at least one of his brothers?

11. Of all the people who have harmed you, consider who is hardest for you to forgive. What, specifically, has made it so hard? Try to answer the question, "If I forgive, then . . ."

12. Help each other evaluate the statements you just made in light of what you've learned in this lesson about the nature of forgiveness. Can you see ways in which you've misunderstood what God requires of you? Discuss any ways in which what you've learned helps you move a step closer to forgiving the person who harmed you.

> *When we forgive it is not just for the sake of others.*
> *Often it is also for our sake.*
>
> ROB PARSONS

Friendship Boosters

1. Take a few moments to exchange phone numbers, addresses, and e-mail addresses (if you have them).

2. On a small slip of paper, write down a statement that expresses a belief you've held about forgiveness that you now see may need to be altered in light of biblical truth. Pair up with the woman on your right and exchange papers. After you've read each other's statements, share how your beliefs have been similar to or different from your partner's. If you have time, briefly swap stories about how the belief you wrote down has caused you confusion, trouble, or heartache in a relationship.

Just for Fun

While studying a subject as serious and sometimes painful as forgiveness, you'll want to help each other keep perspective. No matter what each of you is dealing with in terms of a broken relationship, painful memories, or unresolved guilt, life is also full of beauty, love, and reasons to celebrate. In the week ahead, buy a funny greeting card for the woman you shared with during "Friendship Boosters" and mail it to her. Be part of a "laugh network" with the women in your group so you can keep each other from becoming emotionally bogged down as you continue to explore the important subject at hand.

Praying Together

Come back together as a group and pray that God will give each of you the willingness and courage to embrace what he has to teach you about forgiveness in the weeks ahead. Include a specific prayer for the woman whose paper you're holding: "Lord, help Kathy let go of the assumption that she'll be abused again if she forgives her offender." "God, show Judy that you have a loving plan for her life even though she has been harmed." Affirm together that the love of God is greater than the pain of this world.

> *Laughter is like changing a baby's diaper—*
> *it doesn't permanently solve any problems, but it*
> *makes things more acceptable for a while.*
> BARBARA JOHNSON

Making It Real
in Your Own Life

1. Now that you've gained some insight from the Word and from other women about the nature of forgiveness, review what you wrote in "A Moment for Quiet Reflection." If you are ready to revise any of your beliefs, do so by crossing out words or writing in new ones to clarify your position.

2. Since we have only just begun our study, you probably have nagging questions about forgiveness in general or about how it relates to a specific person in your life. Write down at least three questions and offer them up to God in faith that he will give you helpful insight in the weeks ahead.

> *If any of you lacks wisdom, he should ask God,*
> *who gives generously to all without finding fault,*
> *and it will be given to him.*
>
> JAMES 1:5

Women of Faith Bible Study Series

*Traci Mullins, Judith Couchman, Janet Kobobel
Grant, Evelyn Bence, Beverly Wilson, Phyllis Bennett*

The Women of Faith Bible Study Series helps you turn the laughter and lessons of Women of Faith conferences into a journey of growth shared by special friends. Whether or not you've attended a conference, you will appreciate the bonds that form as you join with other women linked together in friendship, prayer, joy, and faith.

Finding Joy: 0-310-21336-3
Celebrating Friendship: 0-310-21338-X
Embracing Forgiveness: 0-310-21341-X
Experiencing God's Presence: 0-310-21343-6
Growing in Prayer: 0-310-21335-5
Knowing God's Will: 0-310-21339-8
Strengthening Your Faith: 0-310-21337-1
Discovering Your Spiritual Gift: 0-310-21340-1

Pick up a copy today at your favorite bookstore!

GRAND RAPIDS, MICHIGAN 49530 USA

WWW.ZONDERVAN.COM

love

FRUIT OF THE SPIRIT BIBLE STUDIES

SIX STUDIES FOR GROUPS OR INDIVIDUALS

Building Healthy Relationships

Peter Scazzero

**FRUIT OF THE SPIRIT
BIBLE STUDIES**

one

LOVING JESUS

Luke 7:36–50

In the book *Too Busy Not to Pray* Bill Hybels writes, "To people in the fast lane, determined to make it on their own, prayer is an embarrassing interruption. . . . Where does the still, small voice of God fit into our hectic lives? When do we allow him to lead and guide and correct and affirm? And if this seldom or never happens, how can we lead truly authentic Christian lives?"[2]

God calls every believer first to himself and then to ministry. One of the greatest dangers facing us today is our tendency to be so involved in various activities that we lose that "simple and pure devotion to Christ" spoken about by the apostle Paul (2 Cor. 11:3). God wants us to be filled with passion and love for his Son, Jesus Christ.

This story of Jesus and the sinful woman illustrates the kind of simple devotion that God desires.

Warming Up

1.   Think of a person who has "fallen in love." How are his or her attitudes, priorities, and other relationships affected?

---

2 Bill Hybels, *Too Busy Not to Pray* (Downers Grove, Ill.: InterVarsity, 1988), 7, 99.

Digging In

2. Read Luke 7:36–50. How would you describe the setting of this story (the place, the people present, the atmosphere, and so on)?

3. In what ways does the woman demonstrate lavish devotion to Jesus (vv. 36–38)?

4. Imagine yourself at the dinner table. What might you feel during this woman's interruption?

Why do you think her actions offend Simon the Pharisee (v. 39)?

5.   In what ways could we express extravagant devotion to Jesus today?

How might that upset some people around us?

6.   What does it cost this woman to publicly show her love for Jesus?

What are the costs for you?

7. What point does Jesus make for Simon in the parable of the two debtors (vv. 40–43)?

8. Why does Jesus compare Simon's hospitality with that of the woman (vv. 44–46)?

According to Jesus, what does it indicate when a person has little love for him (v. 47)?

9.   What further blessings does the sinful woman receive from Jesus as a result of her faith (vv. 48–50)?

10. With whom do you relate more: Simon the Pharisee, who knows the Bible and is very active for God, or this woman, who is recklessly abandoned to love him? Explain.

11. Why is a passionate love for Jesus so vital if we are to have healthy, loving relationships with others?

12. What obstacles in your life are hindering you from a single-minded devotion to Jesus?

Pray about It

Take a few minutes now to focus your heart and mind on Jesus in prayer, expressing words of affection and adoration to him. Then ask God to help your love for him to be as lavish as his forgiveness.

TAKING THE NEXT STEP

Before a person dies, they often share the concerns greatest on their heart. In John 17 we read Jesus' final words prior to his death. The end of this magnificent prayer climaxes in Jesus praying that the love the Father has for him might be in us. Take time this week to meditate on and memorize John 17:26. Describe the perfect, pure love of the Father toward his Son, Jesus. Imagine yourself loving Jesus with that kind of love. Pray each day in the next week for God to give you the love he has for Jesus. You can be sure God will answer that prayer! He is eager for us to integrate that kind of prayer into our devotional lives.

Fruit of the Spirit

Jacalyn & Stephen Eyre, Jack Kuhatschek, Phyllis LePeau, and Peter Scazzero

The eight-volume Fruit of the Spirit Bible Studies series not only helps you discover what the Bible says about the vital traits that the Holy Spirit produces in believers, but also moves you beyond reflection and discussion to application. Designed for use in small groups or personal devotions, the interactive format will help you grow in your ability to reflect the character of Jesus.

Love: Building Healthy Relationship 0-310-23867-6
Joy: How to Rejoice in Any Situation 0-310-23865-X
Peace: Overcoming Anxiety and Conflict 0-310-23869-2
Patience: The Benefits of Waiting 0-310-23868-4
Kindness: Reaching out to Others 0-310-23866-8
Faithfulness: The Foundation of True Friendship 0-310-23863-3
Gentleness: The Strength of Being Tender 0-310-23864-1
Self-Control: Mastering Our Passions 0-310-23870-6

Pick up a copy today at your favorite bookstore!

ZONDERVAN™

GRAND RAPIDS, MICHIGAN 49530 USA

WWW.ZONDERVAN.COM

Following
Christ's
Example

INTER*Actions*

SMALL GROUP SERIES

LESSONS ON LOVE

SIX SESSIONS

BILL HYBELS

WILLOW CREEK RESOURCES

LOVING LESSONS

THE BIG PICTURE

When a building is being constructed, the groundwork is critically important. If the foundation is faulty, the whole building will be unstable. If the foundation is solid, the building will be stable and stand firm under stress.

The same is true when building loving relationships. We need to have a solid foundation on which to build. If we don't, the whole structure of the relationship is in danger. If we have a solid base of love, we can experience deep and meaningful relationships.

Although all of us desire to be genuinely loving, we all have different natural capacities for receiving and expressing love. If I were to teach a ski class, there would inevitably be a variety of skill levels displayed. Some people would barely be able to stand up. They would be falling over in the lift line, impaling themselves on their ski poles, or accidentally stabbing those around them. Others could negotiate the bunny slope with a certain amount of confidence. And then there would be those who could ski down the hills with ease and style. It doesn't bother us to think about how some people are better at a certain sport or activity. However, when it comes to loving, we assume everyone has acquired the same abilities and skills. The hard truth is that some people have a great natural ability to love, while others have to work at expressing love.

There are a variety of loving capacities among the members of your small group. This may be partly the result of how much love each received in their family as they were growing up. It is also determined by basic temperament and personality. Some of us have soft and gentle temperaments, while others do not.

Our capacity to love is also based on how we have responded to the things life has thrown at us. Life is a mixed bag. Some people encounter obstacles and difficulties and become increasingly bitter and hard-hearted over the years. Others tend to become more open and kind and gentle over time. In almost every group there will be those who are more naturally caring and kind and others who can be short-fused, calloused, and even a little tough-hearted. The majority of us are somewhere in the middle.

A WIDE ANGLE VIEW

1 Put an "X" on each line below to indicate where you would place the following people in relationship to their ability to feel and express love.

Your father

Tenderhearted   Tough-Hearted

|———————————————————————|

Expressive of love   Not expressive of love

|———————————————————————|

Your mother

Tenderhearted   Tough-Hearted

|———————————————————————|

Expressive of love   Not expressive of love

|———————————————————————|

You

Tenderhearted   Tough-Hearted

|———————————————————————|

Expressive of love   Not expressive of love

|———————————————————————|

Why did you choose to put the "X" where you did on each line?

Read Hebrews 10:22–25

2 In this passage we are called to "spur one another on toward love and good deeds." If you view your small group members as the "one another" in this passage, what can you do to "spur one another on" to be more loving?

SHARPENING THE FOCUS

Read Snapshot "You Matter to God!"

YOU MATTER TO GOD!

God wants to see each of us transformed into a more loving person. The first thing He does in this transformation process is convince you, to the core of your being, that you matter to Him. You are the focus of His affection. You are precious in His sight. You are loved beyond words.

When seekers turn to the Bible they find countless portions of Scripture where God takes a huge risk. He knows, with His omniscience, that certain people are going to reject His love, but He says it anyway. I like the way it is put in Isaiah 43, verses 1 and 4. God says through Isaiah, "I have summoned you by name . . . You are precious and honored in my sight." And then there are the words "I love you." In a loveless world, God reaches out and says we matter more to Him than we could ever dream.

---

3 What would you say to a person in your small group to express to them how much they matter to God?

How do we show kids that they matter to God?

Read Snapshot "Love in Action"

LOVE IN ACTION

When it comes to love, God takes it far beyond just words. We all know that talk is cheap. God didn't demonstrate His love in some glittery, Hollywood style with soft colors and moving music in the background. God rolled up His sleeves, put on human flesh, and came to live among us. He became part of a family. He developed a trade as a carpenter. He became active in relationships. He came out of the heavenly grandstand and got knocked around on the playing field of life. This means that when we pray to Him, we can be assured that He knows all about family joys and struggles. He knows all about work. He knows all about relationships. We have rock-solid assurance that He understands. He truly has walked in our shoes.

Another reason God put on human flesh was to show people a purer kind of love than they had ever witnessed before. Love for the unlovely, the needy, the forgotten people, and love for sinners like you and me. Of course, in the supreme demonstration of love, He sacrificed Himself voluntarily and paid the penalty for our sins so that we could come into a relationship with the Father. "Greater love has no one than this, that he lay down his life for his friends" (John 15:13). If you miss this, you miss everything. When you become personally involved with this kind of love, when the scales fall off your eyes for the first time and this kind of love grips you and moves you and comes crashing into your soul, you will never be the same.

4 If you were talking with a seeker who had never stepped foot into a church, how would you explain what God has done to show His love for them?

5 When did you first really experience the depth of God's sacrificial love for you, and what helped you to understand it?

Read Snapshot "The Presence of the Holy Spirit"

THE PRESENCE OF THE HOLY SPIRIT

 Not only does God tell us that we matter to Him, but He also proves His love by His actions. One of the things God has done to show us His love is to send the Holy Spirit to live inside of us. The Holy Spirit assumes the full-time task of warming up your heart and making you a more relational, tender, loving person. When God puts His Holy Spirit in your life, it's like turning a spotlight on a cold, hard heart. The Holy Spirit starts melting you, tenderizing you, making you soft toward God and people. And the good news is that the Holy Spirit will continue to work in you for the rest of your life!

6

How have you experienced the transforming presence and power of the Holy Spirit in the following areas of your life:

- How you love family members

- How you love and care for other followers of Christ

- How you feel toward those who do not yet know God's love

7

What are some of the things you do that limit the impact of the Holy Spirit's power in your life?

What can you do to give the Holy Spirit greater control and room to work in your life?

Read Snapshot "A New Community"

A NEW COMMUNITY

Like it or not, we are deeply impacted by those with whom we spend time. If we are around people who are filled with hate and anger, that hate and anger will eventually begin to infect us. If we are in a community filled with people who know how to love each other, this will also have a transforming effect on our lives. When we become followers of Christ, God places us in a loving community where we are surrounded by people who are diligently seeking to become better at loving.

---

8 If there is a person who is having a negative influence on your life and faith, what can you do to limit their ability to impact your life?

What needs to change in your schedule so that you can spend more time in community with other followers of Christ?

132

9

Picture someone in your life who would benefit from an expression of love from you. What will you do to express your love, and how can the group keep you accountable to this commitment?

PUTTING YOURSELF IN THE PICTURE

YOU MATTER TO GOD

Take time in the coming week to identify two people who need encouragement. Commit yourself to either call them on the phone, write them a letter, or meet with them. Let your primary concern be to communicate to them how much they matter to God. Remind them of what God has done to show His love for them and what Jesus has done to extend forgiveness to them. Also, communicate your love and care for them. Let them know they matter to God and they matter to you.

GROWING IN COMMUNITY

Think of one follower of Christ you know personally who has stopped participating in regular times of worship and Christian community. Contact that person in the coming week and invite them to join you for some kind of gathering of believers.

What changes can you make to create more opportunities for Christian community? Is there an opportunity for deeper fellowship you are not taking advantage of? Spending time with other followers of Christ is essential for our own spiritual growth. What can you do in the coming month to deepen your commitment to developing Christian community?

Bring your group to a deeper level of interaction!
InterActions Series

JOY UNDER PRESSURE

GREAT BOOKS of the BIBLE

PHILIPPIANS

TIM STAFFORD

STUDY 1
BUILDING A FOUNDATION

PHILIPPIANS 1:1–11

When we added on to our home, the extra construction required strengthening the foundation. We live in California, where preparing for earthquakes is a way of life. New, reinforced concrete had to be poured. Steel rods had to be glued into the old foundation, tying old and new together. All this had to be fastened securely to the house through bolts and clips and metal straps. Now when the earth moves, the whole house will bend and flex as a single, strong unit.

People need strong foundations, too. That is why Paul begins this letter the same way he begins most of his other letters: by emphasizing fundamentals. His very emotional words emphasize his ties to the Christians at Philippi and speak of his frequent prayers. There is love here—love that, Paul prays, will grow increasingly intelligent. This loving fellowship, with Christ and each other, can hold these Christians together no matter how the world is shaking.

1. Think of someone who has had a big part to play in your spiritual growth or, conversely, whom you have greatly influenced. What emotions do you feel for that person, and why?

2. Read Philippians 1:1–11. The apostle Paul had an intense spiritual history with the Christians at Philippi. What words does Paul use to describe his attitudes when he prays for them?

3. What attitudes do *you* typically hold when you pray for people?

   If you don't have Paul's attitudes, how can you become more like him?

4. Paul mentions his "confidence" that the Philippians will carry on in their Christian growth (v. 6). What is the root of this confidence?

5. What does Paul mean in saying that the Philippians "share in God's grace with me" (v. 7)?

   Why does this sense of shared grace undergird their mutual love?

6. Often in our "share and prayer" times we concentrate on illness, jobs, and family problems. What does Paul pray for? How can we embrace this as a better model for our prayers?

7. What does Paul mean when he prays that "love may abound more and more in knowledge and depth of insight" (v. 9)?

   Where and how have you seen this kind of love exhibited?

8. We often build friendships on compatibility. We look for people who are likable to us and whom we admire. On what basis does Paul ground his love for the Philippians—on this, or on something else?

9. Suppose there was someone in the Philippian church whom Paul found especially difficult to get along with. What do you think he would do to gain a joyful and loving attitude toward that person?

10. What would it take for you to develop these kinds of attitudes and feelings for other Christians?

What difference would it make in your life if you *did* develop such attitudes and feelings?

Between Studies

During the next week use Paul's prayer for the Philippians as a model for your own prayers. Think especially of a person with whom you have had an intense spiritual connection. (This could be a parent, a spouse, a relative, a friend, or a pastor.) Ask God each day to give that person a more knowledgeable and insightful love as well as discernment for what is really best in his or her life. Ask God to make that person "pure and blameless" and to fill him or her with "the fruit of righteousness." As you think of this person, try to personalize these requests to the circumstances you know he or she deals with.

Great Books of the Bible

Kevin Harney, Walter C. Kaiser Jr.,
Marshall Shelley, Tim Stafford, and Joseph Stowell

The Great Books of the Bible Series explore spiritual wealth, encouragement, and practical wisdom in this collection of 8 foundational and favorite books of the Bible. Six lessons in each guide offer life-changing insights and fresh perspectives on Scripture.

Psalms: Heart to Heart with God 0-310-49871-6
Proverbs: Wisdom for Everyday Life 0-310-49861-9
John: An Intimate Look at the Savior 0-310-49851-1
Romans: Seeing the World Through God's Eyes 0-310-49821-X
Ephesians: Bringing Heaven to Earth 0-310-49841-4
Philippians: Joy Under Pressure 0-310-49811-2
James: Real Faith for the Real World 0-310-49831-7
Revelation: When All Things Become New 0-310-49881-3

Pick up a copy today at your favorite bookstore!

ZONDERVAN™

GRAND RAPIDS, MICHIGAN 49530 USA

WWW.ZONDERVAN.COM

OTC OLD TESTAMENT CHALLENGE 1

CREATING A NEW COMMUNITY

LIFE-CHANGING STORIES FROM THE PENTATEUCH

JOHN ORTBERG
WITH KEVIN & SHERRY HARNEY

God's Greatest Dream

SESSION 1: GENESIS 1 AND 2

Introduction

Words have power!

The things we say and write can change the course of our lives and even history. Consider some of these famous and history-changing words:

I have a dream that one day this nation will rise up and live out the true meaning of its creed: "We hold these truths to be self-evident: that all men are created equal."

I have a dream that one day on the red hills of Georgia the sons of former slaves and the sons of former slave owners will be able to sit down together at a table of brotherhood. . . .

I have a dream that my four children will one day live in a nation where they will not be judged by the color of their skin but by the content of their character. **MARTIN LUTHER KING**
(August 28, 1963, on the steps of the Lincoln Memorial)

Even though large tracts of Europe and many old and famous States have fallen or may fall into the grip of the Gestapo and all the odious apparatus of Nazi rule, we shall not flag or fail. We shall go on to the end, we shall fight in France, we shall fight on the seas and oceans, we shall fight with growing confidence and growing strength in the air, we shall defend our Island, whatever the cost may be, we shall fight on the beaches, we shall fight on the landing grounds, we shall fight in the fields and in the streets, we shall fight in the hills; we shall never surrender. **WINSTON CHURCHILL**
(June 4, 1940, in the British House of Commons)

I am the way and the truth and the life. No one comes to the Father except through me. **JESUS CHRIST**
(John 14:6)

Just as these words had a radical impact on the course of history, so the opening chapters of Genesis introduced words that changed history. The beginning words and themes of Genesis are more countercultural than most of us have ever dreamed.

Looking at Life

1 Describe a time when the words someone wrote or spoke had a dramatic impact on your life.

Learning from the Word
Read: Genesis 1

THE WAY THINGS WERE

To get a sense for how these opening words of Genesis would have hit people in the Old Testament world, you must imagine you lived in those days. You have never heard about a personal God who created all things and who promises life in heaven. This idea has never entered your thinking.

Rather, since you have grown up in the ancient Near East, you have heard a number of stories about how creation took place. None of these stories involves a loving and personal Creator. Rather, they embrace a belief that the universe is filled with many gods who are limited in power, morally fallible, petty, and jealous of each other.

The result of this worldview is that you live in fear and are ruled by superstition. You are in a world with fertility cults that encourage gross sexual immorality. The people around you worship objects like the sun and the moon and even small stone statues. The common belief is that heavenly bodies, like stars, actually influence human affairs.

You perform practices like human sacrifice in an effort to manipulate the gods and gain their favor. Human beings are nothing more than servants created to do the work the gods don't want to do. Life is a cycle of conflict between people and the gods, and in turn, between fellow human beings. Life is not about servanthood but dominance. Immense violence, elimination of the weak, and infanticide are common practices.

The prevailing worldview says that life is just an endless cycle. Life is, in the words of the scholars, "a wheel of life that rotates around the hub of death." One generation is born, grows old, and dies, and another one comes along, and so it goes without any meaning or purpose.

143

Into this horribly destructive belief system these words are spoken: "In the beginning God"—a transcendent, all-powerful, eternal, personal being—"created the heavens and the earth." These words were spoken, and the world has never been the same.

How does Genesis 1 challenge the prevailing worldview of the people who first read these words (as defined in the sidebar "The Way Things Were")?

> 2

What insights do you gain about the character of God from Genesis 1?

> 3

How do you see the distinct persons of the Trinity (Father, Son, and Holy Spirit) working in harmonious partnership in the opening three verses of the Bible?

> God's aim in history is the creation of an inclusive community of loving persons, with Himself included as its primary sustainer and most glorious inhabitant.
>
> —DALLAS WILLARD

Read: Genesis 2:15–25

4

In light of Genesis 1 and 2:15–25, how does God feel about his creation in general and human beings in specific?

How does your perspective on human beings compare with God's?

5

In light of God's view of human beings, respond to *one* of the following questions:

- *How will you be changing a behavior pattern toward one of your family members?*

- *What will you be doing differently in how you relate to a person at work or school?*

- *How will your attitude and behavior change as you relate to a person you don't tend to get along with?*

THE CREATION AND THE CREATOR

God created a place where we could enter into community with him and each other, but we must live with a deep awareness that the Creator and the creation are infinitely different. Though the creation can reveal things about the nature and character of the Creator, the creation must never be worshiped. There is a human tendency to get this confused! In the New Testament, the apostle Paul put it this way: "They exchanged the truth of God for a lie, and worshiped and served created things rather than the Creator—who is forever praised. Amen" (Romans 1:25).

Look at the order of creation and note how God made the sun, the moon, and the stars. In the order of creation, the sun and moon are not spoken into existence until the fourth day. This truth spoke volumes to people who worshiped the heavenly bodies. Genesis teaches that the sun and moon are not divine; they are created objects. They were made by the one God who spoke heaven and earth into existence. Not only does the Bible teach that they have a beginning, but they will also have an end (Revelation 21:23).

A healthy understanding of creation will give us a balanced perspective on material things. We should not be captivated by the stuff of this world, but rather by the One who made it all. Too often in this life, we can become enamored by material things.

What do these opening chapters of Genesis teach you about the relationship between the creation and the Creator?

6

7

Tell about a time when you experienced God's presence and power while in his creation.

How did the beauty and majesty of God's creation move you to give praise to the Creator?

8

Give an example of how we can fall in love with the things of this earth and how they can become more important than God, the one who made them.

9

How can an excessive passion for material things break down our community with God?

Describe a time when you saw this happen in your life.

How can an excessive love of material things erode our community with one another?

10

What do you do to battle against this happening in your life?

The temptation to love the things of this world is illustrated in a painfully clear manner in a magazine ad for a particular car company. The marketing team came up with this slogan:

"You can't buy happiness,
but now you can lease it!"

Genesis gives us a new perspective. We can't buy it, we can't lease it, but God invites us to freely receive what we could never afford.

Old Testament Challenge Volumes 1-4
John Ortberg with Kevin and Sherry Harney

This dynamic program takes your church on an eye-opening, heart-searching journey through Scripture on three interlocking levels:

- Whole congregation—The major themes of the Old Testament snap into focus during 32 weeks of creative and powerful messages that take your entire congregation through the Old Testament.
- Small groups—Truths taught in corporate worship get reinforced through discussion and relationship. Small groups dig deeper into God's Word and apply it to their daily lives.
- Individual—The Scriptures get up-close-and-personal as each participant takes a life-transforming journey through the first two-thirds of the Bible using the *Taking the Old Testament Challenge* individual reading guide.

This threefold approach will drive the truths of Scripture deep into the heart and life of each participant, with applications designed to turn lessons into lifestyles and principles into practice.

Volume 1: Creating a New Community: Life-Changing Stories from the Pentateuch 0-310-24891-4
Volume 2: Stepping Out in Faith: Life-Changing Examples from the History of Israel 0-310-24931-7
Volume 3: Developing a Heart for God: Life-Changing Lessons from the Wisdom Books 0-310-25031-5
Volume 4: Pursuing Spiritual Authenticity: Life-Changing Words from the Prophets 0-310-25142-7
Taking the Old Testament Challenge: A Daily Reading Guide 0-310-24913-9

GRAND RAPIDS, MICHIGAN 49530 USA

WWW.ZONDERVAN.COM

Willow Creek Association

DR. HENRY

CLOUD &

DR. JOHN

TOWNSEND

Authors of the Million-Copy Best-Seller BOUNDARIES

MAKING
SMALL GROUPS
WORK

What Every Small Group Leader
Needs to Know

Chapter 1

God's Surprising Plan for Growth

I will never forget the scene. I (Henry) was doing a training session with seventy-five ministry leaders on how to build small groups that change lives, and they were getting excited about the possibilities. On that particular afternoon I talked about the psychological and relational healing that people experience as they open up with others in a small group. I told of miracles I had seen, and I tried to cast a vision of how life-changing their ministries could be if they learned a few simple concepts.

Then it happened. A guy in the middle of the room just couldn't take it anymore, and he erupted. "I can't allow this to go on any longer!" he said.

"Allow what?" I asked, somewhat taken aback by his interruption.

"This distortion of the Bible," he said. "I can't allow it."

I asked what he meant by "distortion of the Bible." God knows, that is the last thing I would ever want to do, so I wanted to hear him out.

"People grow in one way—through teaching the Bible, preaching the Word of God!" he said. "All this stuff about vulnerability and opening up to each other in groups is not in the Bible. You are distorting the way people grow. We are to teach the Word and let the Bible do its work."

"Well," I said. "Let's see what the Bible itself has to say. Let's see, for example, what Paul thought about 'opening up' to each other." You could feel the tension in the room.

I opened my Bible and read: "We have spoken freely to you, Corinthians, and opened wide our hearts to you. We are not withholding our affection from you, but you are withholding yours from us. As a fair exchange—I speak as to my children—open wide your hearts also" (2 Corinthians 6:11–13).

I went on to read other passages that affirmed the basic power of community and relationships and the New Testament's commands for us to walk in community. I gave an apologetic for how the body of Christ helps us grow. But the man was not buying in so quickly. Instead, he gave me a lesson from his own experience.

"I grew by learning the Bible and walking in the Spirit," he said. "My life changed by learning that one truth. Then when I learned more about the Bible, my life continued to change. I was radically transformed by the Truth. Before that, I was a mess. I was out of control, and a lot was wrong. God changed my life by that one truth."

I know the ministry he was involved in when this all happened. I also know enough about life change to describe what I thought had happened.

"I am sure that learning the Bible and walking in the Spirit were *huge* for you, as they are for all of us in the spiritual life," I said. "I cannot imagine trying to grow or change without those two things. But I also know enough about the ministry you were in to know that other things happened as well.

"You were a college student, floating and lost. You were, as you say, 'out of control.' Then a leader from the ministry reached out and in very real ways befriended you. He told you about God. He taught you some of the truths you are talking about.

"Then he did something else that was key. He invited you to become part of a small group of students that he led. Together you studied the Bible and learned God's transforming truths. But you did much more.

"You also, in that small group, *lived out and experienced those truths.* You opened up to each other about your struggles. You confessed your sins to each other. They offered and helped you feel God's forgiveness. You held each other accountable. When you went through tough times with school or your girlfriend broke up with you, the group supported you, cried with you, and helped you sort it out. They prayed with you, and you sought God together.

"Next they recognized your talents and abilities and encouraged you to use them. They challenged you to take risks, to grow and stretch. In fact, you are probably here today because they pushed you out of your comfort zone more than once.

"When you failed, they comforted you, but did not let you quit. You grew because they encouraged you as your family never did.

"Also, they modeled how to do life. They showed you how to relate and accomplish things in ministry. They let you watch how they did it and then try it for yourself. In that process, you became a lot of who you are today.

"As that community did studies on relationships, you confessed how you fell short in your dating life and you began to treat others differently, starting with them. You learned how to give acceptance and be honest with others—confronting them when necessary, holding them accountable, and being more real than you had ever been.

"I could go on about your involvement with that community and small group, but I think we get the picture. You are right when you say your life was radically transformed. And you are right when you say that God's truth and learning to walk in the Spirit changed your life. But you are wrong when you say that all growth, even your own, comes only from 'teaching and preaching' or learning the Bible. For that is not what the Bible says.

"Your growth also came from the role that the body of Christ, your small group and your leader, played in your life. They delivered the 'goods' you learned about in the Bible. They obeyed what it said to do, and you were the beneficiary.

"Now, the question is, why do you do one thing and say another? Why do you receive those gifts of God and yet tell others that they are to grow some other way? Why do you rob them of what you yourself have experienced and what Paul commanded the Corinthians to do?" I said.

The room was silent. Everyone was reflecting on their own experience of change through spiritual relationships and small group communities. The man I'd addressed just looked at me and then went on with some sort of "yes, but . . ." about the *real value* coming out of teaching and preaching. But he was caught, and the others knew it as well.

The "Say-Do" Gap

I did not really fault the man for his position. He had inherited it from many teachers before him. In fact, he and I met later on and had very good talks. He eventually came around to thinking we were "saying the same thing," as he put it. At least, he began to say that small groups and community are a valid part of the process. Whether or not he would say they are *as valid* as teaching was a little harder for him to do.

But I could understand where he was coming from. It was the "say-do" disconnect. Often, what we say or what we believe is not really what we do or what happens in real life, even when things go well. We say that *one* thing causes growth, when in reality we do *many things* to accomplish that growth. The say-do disconnect is common in the church.

We hold up, and rightly so, Bible study, spiritual disciplines, and direct relationship with God as the paths to spiritual formation. We talk about them, teach on them, practice them, and read books on them, and they slowly become a paradigm in and of themselves of how we grow. And they are vital.

Even so, at the same time, we are doing other things as well. We are connecting with each other, supporting each other, encouraging each other, confessing to each other, and doing a zillion other things the Bible tells us to do in community. All these produce growth, healing, and change. Yet we don't often have a theology for those actions. We do them by happenstance or because our church has decided to "get current" and have some small groups. But we don't hear much biblical teaching on how we grow through connections with other believers in a small group, at least as being a part of doctrine.

In short, while we have a cultural movement of small groups in the church, we often lack a theological vision for their role. Nor do we have practical ways of how to do that vision. We have not given small group processes the weight the New Testament does. As a result, we often experience a stagnated, limited version of being in relationship with God. If by chance we do experience growth through groups, we don't recognize God's role in it. Without a theological vision for growth through small groups, we lose it.

I felt for the man and his limited view that all God does comes through the Bible or direct intervention. I felt also for the people under his teaching. But I was not judging him—because I used to share his view. I had to learn the hard way how God uses small groups and community.

Plan A and Plan B

I went to college with big dreams and expectations. When I was a high school senior, the Southern Methodist University golf coach invited me to Dallas to tour the school and recruit me to come play golf there in the fall. I remember the excitement of playing a U.S. Open course on that trip and dreaming about playing college golf. One week before I left for college, a tendon popped in my left hand. The severe pain abated with cortisone treatments, but it would come back as soon as the medicine wore off. When I got to school, the coach who had recruited me had left, and I was never pain-free long enough to build on my skills. Finally, after two years of struggle, playing well for a while and then poorly, I quit the game that I had dedicated my youth to.

Feeling depressed and bored with my studies, I tried to keep my lost feelings at bay with parties and dating.

One day I was in my dorm room obsessing about my empty life. I could not make the ache go away.

Then something happened that would forever change my life. I looked up on my bookshelf and saw my Bible—the one I had not read since coming to college. I remember thinking, "Maybe something in there would help." So I opened it, and a random verse jumped out at me: "But seek first his kingdom and his righteousness, and all these things will be given to you as well" (Matthew 6:33).

I read it again. "What things?" I asked myself. Then I looked at the whole passage. It was telling me to seek God first and then all these things that I was obsessing about would fall into place.

Was that really true? Was there really a God who could do that? And if he really were there, would he? My thoughts raced as I considered God in a way I never had before. I wasn't just "thinking about God." I was being presented with a defining choice.

I decided to go for it. Sensing the seriousness, I walked across campus and looked for a church. Alone in a dark, empty chapel, I looked up and told God that if he were really there, I would do whatever he told me to do. If he would just show up, I would follow him and do what he said. I waited for him to "zap" me. I waited for a vision. Nothing happened.

I remember feeling a great sense of both relief and emptiness. Relief because after years of playing around with God, I'd come clean and said I would give it all. But empty because I did not sense him there and knew that if he did not show up, I was alone in the universe with nowhere to go and no way to find my way. Doing it on my own had not gotten me very far. I just stared at the ceiling, still wanting him to zap me. Finally I walked back, cold and dreary, to my room.

A while later, the phone rang. It was a fraternity brother. We hadn't talked recently, but he was calling to invite me to a Bible study. I remember his saying that it was strange that he even thought to call me, as I was not overtly into spiritual things. But he felt moved to do it—and I felt as if God was maybe showing up just as I had asked.

Maybe I would go to this Bible study and find God. I thought someone might pray for me, or I would pray, and then God would reach down and finally zap me supernaturally. I would be healed. I would feel good again. I'd find answers to all I was supposed to do. A princess would fall from the sky. After all, I was going the "God route" now, and I expected a miracle.

Well, I did not get my zapping. But I met some new people. Bill, a seminary student, led the Bible study. He and his wife, Julie, opened up their home to me. I decided to take a semester off from school to figure it all out. I moved in with them, and they and another small group became my new spiritual community.

Still depressed and lost, I asked Bill why God did not zap me and make me feel better. His answer—one several people had given as I'd opened up about my feelings—was an answer I was beginning to hate. He said, "Well, sometimes God does that, and he just heals people. But *God uses people, too.*" That was the phrase I hated: *"God uses people, too."*

Bill meant that I had a lot to learn, and he wanted me to "get discipled" and learn about the faith. He also wanted me to get counseling for my depression, another way God uses people. And he thought I should be involved in more spiritual community and relationships. I remember thinking that "God uses people, too" was a "Plan B."

To me, if you were going to get something from God, you should get it "from him," not from people. That was my Plan A—the real spiritual healing, the miracle cure. I thought that when we pray and ask God to heal or to change our lives, he should zap us with a supernatural something. Lightning, earthquakes, visions, or something like that. Knock me down and fix me.

This "God uses people" seemed a spiritual cop-out. If God did not do something, then people had to. So how was that really God? Even if it were God, it was somehow less than the real thing, the zap. But, since I was getting no zapping, I didn't have much of a choice. I got involved in all the small group experiences Bill suggested.

Over the next months, people in my groups loved me, corrected me, confronted me, challenged me, taught me, supported me, and helped heal deep pain and loss. They forgave, accepted, and pushed me. I was learning that I was emotionally disconnected and lacked key relational skills, even though I had a lot of friends. I was not as "real" as I thought I had been. My small group friends taught me that my performance and accomplishments provided a flimsy foundation for measuring my life and my acceptance.

My life was changing through being in a small group, as when the sun comes up in the morning. You don't know exactly when daylight occurs. But you know when it has arrived and that it happened through a process.

One morning I woke and thought, *I am not depressed anymore.* Lying in bed, I pondered how full life had become. I had purpose, meaning, and a new set of talents and abilities the group had encouraged me to pursue. I had new friends and lots of experiences with God. The Bible had become my love. I studied it all the time, and I was having more fun dating than I had without God. Imagine that! All in all, I thought, life is good again. No, not again. In many ways, for the first time. I was full in a way I never had been. And I knew I had God to thank for giving me this new life and all these people who had helped me. I also had another thought, which seems silly now, but gets to the heart of what happened that day I was training those ministers: *I feel good, but I still wish God had healed me. He never did.*

I still thought I had gotten Plan B. In my thinking, the supernatural zap was Plan A, and "God uses people, too" was Plan B. I was healed, but God didn't do it, at least not directly. He did it through people. It was like going to the Super Bowl but sitting in the cheap seats. I saw the game, but not from the box. I got the healing, but not directly from him. I got second best. Still, I was grateful and moved on.

Then one day something happened to further change my life and my understanding of how people grow. I was reading in Ephesians about how we grow into maturity: "From him the whole body, joined and held together by every supporting ligament, grows and builds itself up in love, as each part does its work" (Ephesians 4:16).

I read the verse again. A few thoughts struck me. *From him,* meaning God, *the body,* meaning us, *grows,* meaning changes, as *each part does its work,* meaning that people help each other. That was *exactly* what I had experienced in my own life and what I had seen while working with others. And this passage said it was *from him* that *the body* does these things. It hit me in a new way. What I had called Plan B, God using people, was not a cop-out at all. It was really God's Plan A. He had written right there in the Bible that he planned for his people to grow through people helping people. The body would "build itself up in love." God had healed me after all! Not in some secondary way, but in the way he had intended from the beginning. It was not the cheap seats! This was the fifty-yard line!

Then I began to see this truth all over the pages of the New Testament. God was saying the same thing in many different places: "Each one should use whatever gift he has received to serve others, faithfully administering God's grace in its various forms. If anyone speaks, he should do it as one speaking the very words of God" (1 Peter 4:10–11).

While I had been waiting for God to zap me supernaturally, he had been doing just that. He was zapping me with the love he had put into those around me. He was zapping me with truthful confrontations from those in my group. He was zapping me with healing as they held my hurts and pain. God had been working in the way he designed his body to work—and *it worked.* And that was Plan A all along.

A New Vision

So why do we begin a book on small groups with that lesson? For the same reason I had to have that discussion in the training room of ministers that day. And for the same reason I myself was lost for a long time, thinking that if God was not "zapping" me supernaturally with lightning bolts, then he was not zapping me at all. (By they way, he did do some supernatural zapping as well, just to let you know I believe in that.) We begin with this lesson because so many of us need it and so many of the churches in which you will be leading small groups need it as well.

As we have stated, Paul said the body has work to do if we are going to grow. It is work that only partly happens in a big cathedral-like room on a Sunday morning. Much of that work can't happen in a big room with a lot of people at once. Much of it has to happen in a smaller setting, a more intimate, safer one. One of the best places for this work to happen is in a small group.

What I said earlier is very important. We need to *elevate* the small group process to more than just a "keeping up with the times" way of doing church. Many churches start small group ministries because they see that the churches that are growing have them; they are following the leaders. Many others do it because someone in the church carries the torch for it. Others do it for "special concerns" like recovery or divorce or other areas of focus where people need help.

But no matter why anyone does small groups, one thing should be clear. *Small groups are not an add-on, secondary concern, or fad. What happens in a good small group is part of the very work of the church itself. It is primary, and should be seen that way.* For what you are about to embark on, whether or not your church leadership feels the same way, hold your head high and know that God is very much for the process of his people getting together to help each other grow. It is part of Plan A.

So we want to begin with a new vision for small groups. They are not just culturally relevant for the postmodern world of reality and experienced truth. They are not just a way to be like the "cool" churches. They are not just for the "hurting" people. And they are not just an add-on program. They are a valid expression of what the body of Christ is supposed to be doing on the earth. They are a structured expression of the doctrine of the church. They are as big a part of what the New Testament dictates as preaching and teaching.

So begin there with the knowledge that all of New Testament theology is on your side. God is on your side if you are doing the things in your small group that he tells us to do. And if done well, your church and community are going to be on your side, too, because lives are going to be changed. That is the vision we hope you get for your church, for your leaders, for the people who attend your groups. It is a vision of realizing the total message of the New Testament, one person at a time, one group at a time.

A New Vision with Many Applications

Have you ever known longtime Christians who have significant areas that are not changing? Or they relate to others in ways that are real problems? Have you ever wondered how someone like that can go to church for that many years and not change? What about the person who reads the Bible and knows it better than most, but you can't stand to be around him? What is going on there?

All of us have seen that happen. Most of us have also been that person at one time or another. But what is going on is often no mystery and can be solved. We see the miracle of change over and over again. Once you understand it, things become clear.

What often happens is that someone has been in the faith, doing the disciplines, or attending church, *but has still not been involved in some of the life-changing processes the New Testament commands us to do.* As a result, sometimes change cannot be forthcoming, even with sincere people. But we have seen something else.

Many times these people have never had these New Testament processes offered to them. They have never seen them in practice and have never been taught them. But the Bible is very clear about our need for them. *And, then, when people who have been stuck find themselves involved in a small group that is actually doing the things the Bible says to do in that context, life change occurs that has never before occurred.* That is what we want you to see as well as you embark on the fulfilling role of leading a small group of people further into the realities of life change that God has designed.

You might have a group on basic doctrine or parenting or marriage or recovery from addiction. There are many different kinds of groups. You might be doing a seeker-oriented group designed to introduce people to the things of God for the first time. Or a divorce recovery group or an accountability or prayer group. There are many different applications of the small group process. Our vision is that no matter what kind of group you are doing, certain processes are life changing, and when you implement them to varying degrees, you will see healing and change you never thought possible.

It is to that end we have designed this curriculum. No matter what kind of group you are leading, we think that you can be an instrument of life change for the people who are a part of it. And we don't think that it takes a Ph.D. to do that! We think it takes some basic skills and processes found in the Bible, plus a little dose of love, a mustard seed of faith, some commitment, and an adventuresome spirit. If you have those qualities, you probably have what it takes to facilitate a group that can do what Paul talked about. The group can be an instrument God uses to help others "grow up" in him (Ephesians 4:15). They can learn about God, become better parents, date in more healthy ways, overcome addictions and other recovery issues, heal marriages, and on and on. All because you got a new vision—that God's Plan A is to use you and others to help each other grow.

"SMALL GROUPS ARE SO POWERFUL, AND THE SKILLS REQUIRED
TO LEAD A SMALL GROUP SO LEARNABLE, THAT A LACK OF 'KNOW-HOW'
DOES NOT NEED TO STAND IN THE WAY."
—DR. HENRY CLOUD AND DR. JOHN TOWNSEND

Twenty years of experience has convinced Drs. Cloud and Townsend of the trans-
formative power of small groups. It has also given them keen insight into the two greatest concerns of pastors, church leaders, and small group leaders: *How do we get leaders?*
and *How do we train them?*

MAKING **SMALL GROUPS** WORK responds by showing group leaders how to
lead the kinds of groups that realize their full, life-changing potential. Whether the group
is a Bible study, support group, or a group designed for a specific area of life, you'll learn skills
and biblical processes that can help your people grow together.

Discover how you can help a group of any kind move beyond a *small* group to a
growth group. This book will help you
❧ decide on the type of group and its purpose ❧
❧ create and maintain safety ❧ choose the best materials ❧
❧ establish ground rules and maintain balance ❧
❧ facilitate deeper group process that brings about life change ❧
❧ know the difference between the leader's roles, and the members' roles ❧
❧ deal with difficult issues and those challenging members
who often hinder the group's experience ❧
❧ develop the gifts of group members . . . and more. ❧

Dr. Henry Cloud and Dr. John Townsend are popular speakers and cohosts of the nationally
broadcast *New Life Live!* radio program. They are best-selling coauthors of several books, including *Boundaries with Kids, Boundaries in Dating, How People Grow, The Mom Factor, Safe People,
Twelve "Christian" Beliefs That Can Drive You Crazy*, and the Gold Medallion Award-winning
Boundaries and *Boundaries in Marriage*.

Cover design: Holli Leegwater / Cover photo: Minoru Toi/Photonica
CHURCH AND MINISTRY / MINISTRY RESOURCES / SMALL GROUP

US $14.99/ $22.99 CAN
ISBN 0-310-25028-5

51499

9 780310 250289   EAN

WWW.ZONDERVAN.COM

LEADING

LIFE-CHANGING

small groups

BILL DONAHUE

and the WILLOW CREEK SMALL GROUPS TEAM

Mission, Values, and Vision

Mission Statement and Ministry Philosophy for Small Groups

A mission statement and ministry philosophy are key to the success of your ministry because they function as navigational tools necessary to chart an accurate course toward a worthy destination. The statement used to launch small group ministry of Willow Creek Community Church in South Barrington, Illinois, serves as an example. Below, and on the following pages, you'll find our view of small groups outlined and explained. As you read it, consider how you might shape and articulate *your* church's vision and values.

The overriding mission at Willow Creek is to "turn irreligious people into fully devoted followers of Christ." In order to accomplish that mission, a variety of ministries exist at Willow Creek. From the weekend service to the midweek New Community believer's service to the various subministries throughout Willow Creek, we are committed to moving people toward Christlikeness. Since small groups have become our way of doing ministry, it is essential that we understand the role they play in carrying out our overall mission.

Below, you will notice the mission statement for the purpose of small groups at Willow Creek and how small groups are used to accomplish our overriding mission. The questions "Why do small groups exist?" and "For what purpose do small groups exist?" are answered in the mission statement. Following the mission

---

Mission: Building a Community to Reach a Community

To connect people into groups of four to ten who come together on a regular basis for a common purpose and are led by an identified leader who is assisting them in their progress toward full devotion to Christ by intentionally providing an environment for connection, community, and spiritual formation.

statement you will find a philosophy of ministry structured around five key values we believe will shape the way Willow Creek does ministry for the coming years. These five statements are beliefs or values, based on Scripture, that undergird our ministry philosophy.

5 Core Values

▶ Mandate: Spiritual Transformation

"...I have set you an example that you should do as I have done for you."

John 13:15

Other Scriptures:
John 14:15
Romans 6:12–13, 17–19; 8:29
Philippians 1:6
Colossians 1:28; 2:6–7
1 John 2:6

Jesus Christ, as Head of the church, intends His followers to become like Him

It is God's plan that those who call on His name should be like Him in attitude and behavior. The church exists not just to collect followers, but to transform them.

Church life is the sum of all the activities that promote Christ's work of transformation. Programs and subministries in a church should be designed to serve His goal of changing lives, and should be surrendered as obsolete when they fail to achieve this end.

We describe the life change the church exists to produce with "The Five G's": *Grace* (to personally appropriate and extend the saving work of Christ), *Growth* (pursuing Christlikeness), *Group* (connecting with others in significant relationships), *Gifts* (serving Christ's body according to spiritual giftedness and passion), and *Good stewardship* (honoring God with our resources through what we give to the church and what we keep).

The Five G's				
Grace	*Growth*	*Group*	*Gifts*	*Good Stewardship*

▶ Method: Small Group Community

"He appointed twelve— designating them apostles—that they might be with him."

Mark 3:14

Other Scriptures:
Exodus 18:17–27
Acts 2:46

A small group provides the optimal environment for the life change Jesus Christ intends for every believer

Significant relationships (including one-to-one) occur best in the context of a small group. Connecting people in a small group is not an optional subministry of the church—it is essential for growth. Without this connection, people can, at best, attend meetings, but they aren't truly participating in church.

A small group of believers who love one another with God's love will experience the life Christ promised at the deepest level possible. This love radically transforms them and demonstrates His power. A group that by design does not contribute to this goal of spiritual maturity may well be a collection of Christians, but it is not a successful small group.

A variety of small groups are necessary to meet the individual needs of believers, as well as the diverse needs of the body as a whole. People can grow in Christlikeness, care for each other, and make a contribution in any group, whether it be a disciplemaking group, task group, nurture group, Christian twelve-step group, counseling group, or any other type. However, ministries in a local church that don't have small groups built into their structure generally can't produce optimal life change for people looking to that ministry for growth and service opportunities.

▶ Mobilize: Strategic Leaders

The most strategic person in the life-change process of the church is the small group leader

The priority of church leadership is to help small group leaders succeed through support and training. To that end, the best resources of the church should be employed to make sure the small group leader has everything necessary for effectiveness.

Small group leaders cannot flourish in a vacuum. Leaders need to band together periodically with other leaders for encouragement and accountability (huddling). Additionally, church staff and other leaders must provide training in skills necessary for group life (skill training) and reminders of the purpose and goals that drive the ministry (vision casting). Basic skills necessary for effective leadership of a small group are the same whether one is leading a task group of volunteers, a youth team, or a couples small group.

Leaders need oversight from coaches who can offer them encouragement and accountability. Coaches should not violate an appropriate span of care (1 coach for every 4–5 leaders). This holds true throughout the entire church—everyone must be cared for by someone.

The ultimate goal of a leader is life change: to help group members grow in Christlike character through learning, loving one another, and contributing of themselves and their resources. Yet leaders must also help their groups grow in size and eventually birth new groups. (We acknowledge that some groups are closed to address specific issues or cover a specific curriculum.) The leader takes responsibility for this growth by recruiting an apprentice, attending training, and by planning for the eventual birthing process.

▶ Multiply: Span of Care

Groups must expand and multiply so that eventually every believer can be connected to others

A small group does not ultimately exist for itself. Christlike people resist the urge to be selfish—they desire to include other unconnected people in such a way that they too may experience group life. Small groups therefore must have a viable strategy for growth and reproduction so that someday everyone who gathers as a part of the local church is included in some kind of identifiable relational connection.

Apprenticeship fosters new leaders and must be an integral part of group life so that emerging leaders continually gain on-the-job experience and can be ready to lead groups of their own as soon as they are ready.

"It was he who gave some to be apostles, some to be prophets, some to be evangelists, and some to be pastors and teachers, to prepare God's people [average believers] for works of service."
Ephesians 4:11–12

Other Scriptures:
1 Corinthians 16:15–16
1 Thessalonians 5:12–13
Hebrews 13:7, 17

"And the things you have heard me say . . . entrust to reliable men who will also be qualified to teach others."
2 Timothy 2:2

Other Scriptures:
Matthew 9:36–38;
29:19–20
Acts 1:8

When a group gets too large, its leader cannot provide the care necessary for life transformation of each individual. Though groups must grow, the appropriate span of care of approximately one leader for every ten people needs to be maintained. The next step for groups that grow above ten members is to birth new groups.

Success in leadership of a small group is ultimately seen in the viability of daughter groups. The goal is not just to start a new group, but to birth a group that is healthy and creates life change. The new group can only be considered viable if it eventually births a new group itself. In this model, a senior leader is someone who's birthed additional groups, which in turn have birthed new groups—in other words, a leader with small group "grandchildren."

"And the disciples were filled with joy and with the Holy Spirit."

Acts 13:52

Other Scriptures:
Nehemiah 8:9–12
Acts 2:46–47; 8:4–8
Luke 10:17, 21

► Means: Seek and Celebrate

Effective ministry happens in an atmosphere of prayer and celebration

God is sovereign, and He sovereignly declares that we should pray. Great ministry follows great praying—believers who talk to their heavenly Father receive because they ask; when they knock, He opens. Leaders are to pray as Jesus prayed: publicly as well as privately, authentically as well as powerfully, specifically as well as continually. Those who seek God's blessing on their work must seek His presence in their work through prayer.

Observe, share, value, and celebrate God's activity. A climate of fun and festivity should permeate gatherings related to ministries.

Leadership successes should be a source of public as well as private rejoicing. Small group gatherings do not take the place of many people coming together for public exaltation of God, catalytic teaching of scripture, and telling stories about what He is doing among the members of the church in small groups. What happens at the small group level should transform the large gathering, and vice versa.

Developing Fully Devoted Followers

The ultimate purpose of small groups is to move people toward a greater relationship with Christ and to transform them into His image. But often the question is asked, "What does it mean to be like Jesus?" Below, you will see how we define a follower of Christ in terms of the local church. As you read, think first about your own development. Then, decide how you will develop as Christ followers in your church.

"A student is not above his teacher, nor a servant above his master. It is enough for the student to be like his teacher, and the servant like his master."

Matthew 10:24–25

► What Is a Disciple?

In the simplest form, a disciple is an apprentice to Jesus

At Willow Creek we define discipleship as "living as Christ would if He were in my place." Discipleship—in these broad terms—implies a life of transformation and dependence on the Holy Spirit.

▶ How Does a Disciple Function in the Local Church?

With the definition of a disciple in hand, let's describe the activity of one in and through the local church. As one functions as a Christ-follower in church, one becomes a "participating member" of that local body. A participating member at Willow Creek (that is, a Christ follower or disciple) is described as one who is maturing in grace, growth, group, gifts, and good stewardship. Our elders have shaped them this way: grace, growth, group, gifts, and good stewardship.

Grace

Christ followers understand and have individually received Christ's saving grace. They have abandoned all attempts to earn God's favor through accomplishments of their own and find security only through Christ's sacrificial death on their behalf.

In obedience to Christ's command, they have undergone water baptism as believers, giving outward witness to the inner cleansing and renewal experienced in Him.

Christ followers also desire to extend the grace they've received to others through personal evangelism and participation in the collective ministry of the church in their community, their country, and around the world.

The individual appropriation of the saving work of Christ.
Ephesians 2:8–9

Growth

Christ followers know that the grace of God that saved them is only the beginning of His work in them. They gratefully respond by actively pursuing a lifelong process of spiritual growth in Christ and by seeking to become conformed to His image. To this end, they consistently nurture their spiritual development through prayer, worship, and Bible study.

They regard the Bible as the final authority in all areas that it teaches about and desire to be wholly obedient to it. Christ followers honestly confront areas of personal sin and engage the Holy Spirit's power in seeking to turn from sin.

The ongoing evidence of a changing life in pursuit of Christlikeness.
2 Peter 3:18

Group

A Christ follower honors God's call to participate in community in order to grow in Christlikeness, express and receive love, and carry out the ministry of the church.

For this reason, they give priority to attending the corporate gatherings of the church for the purpose of worship, teaching, and participation in the sacrament of communion, and are connected relationally to a small group for the purpose of mutual encouragement, support, and accountability.

Christ followers also

- pursue Christ-honoring relationships at home, within the church, and in the marketplace, and are committed to pursuing the biblical pattern of reconciliation when conflict arises;

- support the leadership of the church and are biblically submissive to it;

- affirm and uphold the fundamental truths of Scripture (as summarized in our Statement of Faith) and refrain from promoting other doctrines in ways that cause dissension.

Connections with others in significant relationships.
Acts 2:46

Gifts

Serving Christ's body according to spiritual giftedness and passion.

Romans 12:6–8

Christ followers recognize that the church is composed of interdependent members, each uniquely gifted by the Holy Spirit for the purpose of building up the body and furthering the ministry of the church. They therefore seek to discover, develop, and deploy those God-given gifts and to seek a place of service within the church with the support and affirmation of the body.

Good stewardship

Honoring God financially through what we give to the church and what we keep.

Philippians 4:11–19

Christ followers realize they have been bought with the price of Christ's blood, and that everything they are and have belongs to Him.

In light of this, they desire to be responsible caretakers of the material resources with which God has entrusted them. They recognize the tithe (ten percent of one's earnings) as the historical standard of giving in Scripture. But, moreover, in response to Christ's abundant giving, they increasingly submit their resources to His lordship and display a spirit of generosity and cheerfulness in supporting the work of the church and reaching out, with compassion, to a needy world.

Vision for Small Groups

Here is our vision for the small group effort at Willow Creek:

> ## To become a church where nobody stands alone.

We want our people to know that we want to become something—a place where there is always a seat at the table of community. We are the body of Christ, the family of God, a community of followers devoted to Christ and His cause. So let's get a better grip on what this "community" is and why we want to see the entire church come together in little communities.

▶ Small Groups in the New Testament

Community is a theme that runs throughout Scripture. God has always been calling out a people for Himself, beginning with Israel and continuing with the church. Even when the Jews were dispersed among enemy nations during times of captivity, they organized themselves into groups and ultimately formed synagogues (Jewish communities of worship and teaching), where they could serve one another and carry out their beliefs. It was natural, therefore, for Jesus to develop a community of followers and for Paul, Peter, and other church planters to start new communities wherever they went as they proclaimed the Gospel. These new communities began as small groups, just as Jesus had modeled with the twelve disciples (Mark 3:14; Luke 6:12–19).

Small groups were an integral part of the early church structure. They were small enough to allow individual members to minister to one another, use their spiritual gifts, and be discipled in the teachings of Christ. In addition, they were vibrant and life-giving communities where evangelism could take place as unchurched people watched a loving and compassionate community in action. Small groups not only built up the church as the first living examples of biblical community but were vehicles for reaching a lost world for Christ.

▶ What Is Biblical Community?

Defining community may be more difficult than practicing it. So, for the sake of simplicity, here is a broad working definition.

Definition of Biblical Community:

"Christian Community is the body of Christ expressing the life and message of Christ to build up one another and redeem the world for God's glory."

The new community that formed on the Day of Pentecost immediately began to function in small groups. These groups wholeheartedly devoted themselves to the teaching of the apostles, to fellowship with one another, to practicing the Lord's Supper together, and to praying for one another. These new communities were characterized by mutuality, accountability, servanthood, love, and evangelism.

Small groups are a place of mutual ministry among members. Each member uses spiritual gifts to serve other members in the body. Mutual ministry is a trademark of a Christ-following community or small group.

A small group gathers together to provide fellowship and mutual support so that the church can have an impact in their community. They encourage and build up one another so that the body of Christ can be cared for and the world can be influenced through their good deeds.

Small groups exist to teach the truth and develop future leaders who can shepherd others and disciple them in the faith. For this purpose, each leader, or coach, has an apprentice he or she is developing toward greater responsibility and leadership.

Mission, Values, and Vision matter. Making devoted followers of Christ in a biblical community is the purpose of the church. Once this is clear, you can begin to build a structure that will foster these ideals.

"Every day they continued to meet together in the temple courts. They broke bread in their homes and ate together with glad and sincere hearts, praising God and enjoying the favor of all the people."

Acts 2:46–47

"Now to each one the manifestation of the Spirit is given for the common good."

1 Corinthians 12:7

"And let us consider how we may spur one another on toward love and good deeds. Let us not give up meeting together, as some are in the habit of doing, but let us encourage one another—and all the more as you see the Day approaching."

Hebrews 10:24–25

"And the things you have heard me say . . . entrust to reliable men who will also be qualified to teach others."

2 Timothy 2:2

171

THE BEST-SELLING SMALL GROUP GUIDEBOOK
OVER **100,000** COPIES SOLD
NOW UPDATED

Like nothing else, small groups have the power to change lives. They're the ideal route to discipleship—a place where the rubber of biblical truth meets the road of human relationships.

For six years Bill Donahue provided training and resources for small group leaders so that Willow Creek could build a church of small groups. Now he is committed to creating tools that will help church leaders pursue the same goal—to provide a place in community for everyone in their congregation. In *Leading Life-Changing Small Groups*, Donahue and his team share in depth the practical insights that have made Willow Creek's small group ministry so effective.

the comprehensive, ready-reference guide
for small group leaders

The unique, ready-reference format of this book gives small group leaders, pastors, church leaders, educators, and counselors a commanding grasp of:

- Group formation and values
- Leadership requirements and responsibilities
- The philosophy and structure of small groups
- Meeting preparation and participation
- Discipleship within the group
- Leadership training . . . and much more

From an individual group to an entire small group ministry, *Leading Life-Changing Small Groups* gives you the comprehensive guidance you need to cultivate life-changing small groups . . . and growing, fruitful followers of Christ.

> *By far the most comprehensive how-to manual for small groups yet to be developed. Bill Donahue is America's leading authority on small groups, and in this book he freely shares from his years of experience.*
> — **TIM WAY,** Senior Buyer, Books, Family Christian Stores

> *The most complete and comprehensive tool for training small group leaders available. It carries my highest recommendation.*
> — **GARETH ICENOGLE, D.MIN.,** Pasadena International Small Group Consultant; Adjunct Professor, Fuller Seminary

> *The best material I have found for delivering a comprehensive training curriculum. Set it in front of small group leaders and immediately there is something they can use.*
> — **JON WALLACE,** Senior Vice President, Azusa Pacific University

BILL DONAHUE, Ph.D., is Executive Director of Small Group Ministries for the Willow Creek Association. He previously served on the staff of Willow Creek Community Church, helping to develop and launch the church-wide small group ministry. Coauthor with Russ Robinson of *Building a Church of Small Groups* and *The Seven Deadly Sins of Small Group Ministry*, he has edited or contributed to many Willow Creek small group Bible study guides, including the Interactions and New Community series. He currently leads a small group and lives in West Dundee, Illinois, with his wife, Gail, and their two children.

Cover design: Rob Monacelli
Cover photos: Eyewire

CHURCH AND MINISTRY / MINISTRY RESOURCES / SMALL GROUP

ZONDERVAN™
WWW.ZONDERVAN.COM

WILLOW CREEK RESOURCES
www.willowcreek.com

US $16.99 / $25.99 CAN
ISBN 0-310-24750-0

9 780310 247500   51699

Bill DONAHUE   Russ ROBINSON

meeting the challenges
every group faces

walking the small group
TIGHTROPE

some problems can't be solved

AN INTRODUCTION
TO POLARITY MANAGEMENT

We have been leading or participating in small groups for a combined total of over fifty years. Wow! That makes us feel old, especially with a certain "magic birthday" looming on the horizon for both of us. The two of us have accumulated enough time in the small group leader saddle that you might think we would have figured it all out by now.

Guess again.

Don't get us wrong. We have definitely had our share of small group highs. Some of them even happened when we were leading! But our past is checkered with a considerable number of small group lows.

Good Agendas Gone Bad

I (Bill) remember taking a couples' group on an overnight retreat to spend some focused time on our marriages. It was the ideal setting—a beautiful lake, a private home with water toys and rafts, and two full days together, building community amidst God's glorious creation. There was only one small problem — one very small, whining, crying, screaming, burping problem. The kind with a built-in alarm that goes off at 2 A.M.... and 3 A.M.... and 4 A.M. The kind of problem that challenges everyone's sanctification. Against my better judgment, I had allowed one couple to bring little Johnny along. After the first night, I found myself wanting to write a children's book called *How to Help Little Johnny Sleep through the Night (and 99 Other Uses for Duct Tape).*

When we tried to gather as a group, it was clear that Johnny's parents were exhausted, group members were annoyed, and the atmosphere was becoming tumultuous. But that didn't stop me from pushing ahead with my agenda. *After all, what's more important — the people or the agenda?*

Using my extensive powers of observation, I asked, "So how's everyone doing? Have you been able to spend some quality time relaxing and talking about your marriage relationships?" Eight sets of eyes focused on me like a foray of heat-seeking missiles. (I couldn't see the ninth set, because my wife was sitting next to me.) Nervous from the response, I unwisely asked a follow-up question. "Scott and Janet, you have been working on your communication together. Uh, how's that going?" Looking back, I should have suggested we all watch a video.

Janet began to cry, while Scott sat motionless and avoided all eye contact. It was painfully uncomfortable and awkward. A perceptive leader would have seen it coming, recognizing not only the couple's tension but also the group's discomfort. Instead of offering friendship and compassion, I provided accountability and called people to accomplish "the mission at hand." Thankfully, by God's grace and with kind input from a few members, we salvaged the weekend and created some memorable moments. But my inability to read the group in that moment almost compromised the community we'd been trying to build together.

I (Russ) misplayed a hand I was dealt just a few years ago in a couples' group Lynn and I were leading. The timing was ironic; I had just been invited to become Willow Creek's director of small groups, a position that would have me eventually guiding a ministry with over 3,500 small group leaders and staff! You would think I wouldn't goof up common-sense relationship dynamics at this stage of my leadership. But I did.

One of the couples in our group started having "marital challenges," a euphemism we use to disguise the relational crisis at hand and pretend it is not serious. We knew danger was lurking around the next bend but tried to ignore it at first. Before long, the couple's marital frustrations began to seep through routine answers to discussion questions, and it was clear they needed help. As they periodically sought our counsel, Lynn and I tried to help them lessen some symptoms of their problems but remained somewhat ignorant and too busy to see the issues for what they really were.

As more of the couple's relational toxins spilled into our group's meetings, we worried about saying anything to the group, fearing it would violate the couple's confidence. But our silence was like throwing a blanket over the proverbial elephant in the room, thinking no one would notice. Unfortunately, this elephant was gaining weight — and fast! Our conclusion? We decided to confront the couple about how their interpersonal conflict was ruining the entire group dynamic.

Well, you can imagine the ensuing train wreck. They were devastated and lashed back with feelings of disappointment and betrayal. In their view, we had responded in glib and superficial ways to their problems and had failed to show them earlier how their behavior was impacting the group. They felt exposed, wounded, and devalued.

Of course, being the spiritual giants we are, we became defensive. We pointed out their unwillingness to seek professional help and insisted they keep their marital problems to themselves during group discussions, unless they were willing to bring the whole sorry tale before the entire group.

(I'm so embarrassed as I write this. What were we thinking?)

Group momentum and growth deteriorated considerably in the coming months, and what had begun as a dream of deeper community turned out to be a nightmare for our group. When the group finally ended, we were drained but relieved. We never really resolved our leadership miscues until many months later. We are grateful that treasured friendships were reconciled, mostly through the grace of couples who chose to focus on what good we did provide them.

But this experience was a confidence rattler for Lynn and me. We thought we had done all the things good small group leaders do. Our review confirmed that most of our moves were by the book. We'd received solid training that helped us foster much good in that little community. But it had all gotten off the rails so easily and quickly. Perhaps we had overlooked something.

"All Learning Comes from Failed Experience"

Despite many successful group experiences filled with rich community and spiritual transformation, some group failures stumped us. From time to time we'd swap personal stories as well as those of other groups that had hit a wall. And we'd wonder if there were common sticking points or mistakes that could be avoided, thus helping groups move forward.

Neither of us wanted to admit what we knew was true. *It wasn't supposed to happen this way! Why did some groups have a wonderful, life-changing experience while others seemed to wander, drift, or just blow up?*

These thoughts were especially troubling for us because we had read so many small group resources and had availed ourselves of loads of training. Our leadership roles have afforded us the opportunity to sit among the best and the brightest when it comes to community building, personal transformation, and group life. And we have grown and changed as a result. But we knew we were still missing some pieces of the puzzle.

Our failures paved the way for fresh insights into how churches and small groups provide members with a transformational experience in community. An unexpected twist revealed our failures as opportunities to learn.

Our leadership team attended a seminar on creative learning strategies, and during introductory comments, the trainer posed what seemed a simple dilemma: "When do people learn?" After we'd provided several inadequate solutions, the trainer rescued us with this simple but profound observation: "When they fail. All learning comes from failed experience." When experience fails to match expectations, the dissonance produces the energy for learning, discovery, and change.

Those words became a kind of mantra for us, stimulating fresh thinking and moving our focus from how badly we had failed to how much we could learn from our failures. This freeing perspective allowed us to realize we had missed some key group dynamics in our understanding and training. It was clear we needed to change how we thought about community life and leadership.

The basic leadership training program we had created was good. Clarity on the fundamentals of small group leadership still mattered. So we remained committed to the tools and training materials we had developed, many of them contained in *Leading Life-Changing Small Groups.*[1] But we knew we were ready to learn more. Thankfully, that learning also came from an unexpected source.

The "Aha" Moment

I (Russ) was having lunch at Willow Creek one day with Wayne Alguire, former Levi Strauss executive and then Willow Creek Association staff member. (Wayne is now the lead pastor of one of Willow's new regional campus sites). Since I was an attorney, and he a corporate executive, our work with Willow sometimes involved legal matters and organizational concerns of the church and Willow Creek Association. Wayne is a voracious reader, so I asked what he'd been reading.

"I'm rereading a favorite from my Levi Strauss days called *Polarity Management,* by Barry Johnson," he remarked.[2] He went on to explain how this book had helped him solve some business problems. For example, how can a business make customers happy and yet produce a profit? Or are these challenges mutually exclusive? Do leaders have to choose between making money and customer satisfaction? Are we here to please shareholders or customers?

In today's business environment, as many of you know, there is no choice; both must be accomplished, or you are out of business. In fact, you have to *exceed* customer expectations and turn them into raving fans. But along the way, you had better make enough profit to pay generous bonuses, overwhelm your lenders, and thrill shareholders at the annual meeting, or you may wind up refurbishing your resume.

Many businesspeople spend an inordinate amount of time trying to find "the answer" to do both things at once. Johnson suggests that maybe there's no magic solution for doing both in business. Rather, they exist in a dynamic tension that a business owner must manage.

My discussion with Wayne gave me an "aha" moment. I immediately started thinking about how this concept applied to many areas, from parenting to church life to small groups. For example, parents have two main jobs. (Actually, therapists agree that parents have 5,493,671 jobs to do. We are focusing on just two to make a point.)

One job is to create a nurturing environment that enfolds children in a safe, healthy family that sticks together through thick and thin. But parents also have to develop their children so they can eventually leave the nest and enter the world's stark realities. The objective is to achieve this by a reasonable age. (For parents, that's 16; for kids, it's 27.) These two worthy goals — forming a close-knit family and developing competent, independent young adults — appear to contradict each other. If you're a parent, you know the tension you live with, especially as your children age, to both embrace and release them — to hold two good things in tension with one another.

Consider the church. We want to reach lost people — missions and evangelism. But we must also meet believers' needs — care and discipleship. It all sounds so straightforward when Jesus says, "Therefore go and make disciples of all nations, baptizing them in the name of the Father and of the Son and of the Holy Spirit, and teaching them to obey everything I have commanded you" (Matt. 28:19–20). Churches have spent two thousand years trying to figure out how to keep both purposes alive, though they appear to tug against one another.

Churches like ours have made the Great Commission a passion, seeking to turn irreligious people into fully devoted followers of Christ. And we have come to recognize the tensions that arise when you allocate staff energy, church resources, and volunteer efforts to the cause. Churches must decide whether the next dollar in the offering plate will support evangelism or discipleship, be strategically invested in the missions ministry agenda or in the Christian education department. Do we put more resources toward reaching skeptics or building up saints? Yet again, two good things stand in tension with each other.

If you subscribe to polarity management theory, it's okay to say sometimes, "There is no answer to that question."

The principles of polarity management suggest that in every area of life we must learn to manage the tension between two good things rather than choose one thing over another. Business leaders strive to make a profit *and* please customers. Good parents make every effort to build close, interdependent relationships with their kids *and* prepare them to live independently when they are grown. Churches must evangelize *and* disciple. In these situations, choosing one thing over another is not an option; we must do both.

The more you understand this principle and observe the world around you, the more often you will spot the examples of this principle. Not every hard-to-solve problem can be stated in terms of polarity. Sometimes a challenge demands more focused attention, further experimentation, and increased creativity. But often when a problem seems intractable or extensive work results in failure, we are missing the obvious.

Johnson's insights were eye opening, but further reflection made us realize how he has simply creatively described what Scripture has always told us. There are many polarities in the kingdom. Jesus called the Twelve to be with him, so that he could send them out (Mark 3:14). Paul reminds us "there is one body and one Spirit ... one lord, one faith, one baptism; one God and Father of all.... *But to each one of us* grace has been given" (Eph. 4:4–7, italics ours). Paul continues by listing individual gifts and ministries. In fact, each one's uniqueness in Christ is the very thing that eternally binds us interdependently to the body as a whole. A community that deplores individuality produces communism. An individual who ignores community embraces narcissism.

Certainly the greatest tension of all time remains an enigma for theologians of every persuasion: reconciling man's free will and God's absolute sovereignty. So Paul can say, "I have become all things to all men so that by all possible means I might save some" (1 Cor. 9:22). Sounds like Paul thinks the whole salvation enterprise depends on his efforts, tact, and ability to accommodate the culture. And yet, regarding salvation and election, in Romans 9 he emphatically states, "It does not, therefore, depend on man's desire or effort, but on God's mercy" (v. 16). Some churches favor the Paul of 1 Corinthians 9, and others the Paul of Romans 9. Both statements reflect a truth in the kingdom and must be held in a dynamic tension. To favor one leads to complacency in evangelism; to favor the other makes us self-glorifying idolaters.

And that's the fundamental benefit behind polarity management. Instead of looking for right answers and nice little definitions, sometimes it's better to identify and manage the tensions that exist between two desirable truths or outcomes. In fact, Johnson actually calls them "unsolvable problems." Good phrase. Makes us sleep better at night!

After learning more about polarity management, we simplified its principles considerably. (This is a fascinating field of study, but we concluded it would be best to use its concepts in distilled form.) Then we applied our learning to small group life as we continued to lead groups. Finally, we began to teach it to small group leaders at Willow Creek and elsewhere.

Once you recognize the benefits of holding two good things in tension, your future gets a little easier to manage. Instead of fighting the tension, you can use it to your advantage. Managing tension keeps things in balance. A trampoline works because it utilizes gravity and elasticity. One without the other would be disastrous.

Ask any tightrope walker. A nice taut rope, stretched appropriately between two good places — the start and the finish — makes for an exciting act. To loosen the rope at either end renders the task impossible. It is the tension that produces results, and an informed and capable walker learns to manage it to his or her advantage. So much of life is the same. Yes, life really is a circus sometimes, and you get to play the tightrope walker.

No Paint by Numbers

Suddenly we realized that what we had previously classified as failures were unseen and unsolvable problems. As we began to apply more of the polarity concept to small groups, things became clearer.

Much teaching in Christian circles implies that if you simply do A, B, C, and D, you will have an abundant life, or become wealthy, or unlock hidden secrets to incredible living, or master biblical community, or avoid financial ruin, or have a powerful prayer experience, or never get cancer, or have a great small group! The problem? We have had small groups in which we've done A, B, C, and D (and even E, F, and G), and guess what? It wasn't so great a small group. Why? Life happens. People sin. The world is a mess.

And the real kicker was, we'd been in or seen other groups in which leaders fumbled and bumbled around, ignoring B and D and doing C before A, and yet ended up with a better experience than others. Now what's up with that? If you fail on A through G, why don't you automatically end up with a bad small group?

Painting by numbers may help organize your color patterns, but it will not produce a life-giving work of art. And leading a small group is more about art than about painting by numbers.

We discovered that it is still essential to know the basics, just as it is in any field or discipline, whether art, music, or auto repair. Understanding A through G (and maybe Z!) matters, but it isn't an automatic formula for success any more than knowing how to use a hammer makes me a carpenter. Every leader should learn how to give people a sense of belonging, help them wrestle with Scripture, lead a good discussion, create a loving environment, and listen carefully to members' needs. Nothing we say in this book undermines the fundamentals of good shepherding.

But as important as all those things are, we stumbled into a second truth, and it is the core of this book. Small group leadership is not a paint-by-numbers exercise in which you'll get a beautiful picture by simply putting the right color on the right number. It really is more of an art — an acrobatic art, if you will. It is the art of managing the dynamic tensions that constantly exist in the context of every group. Entering into the life of a little community requires its participants be aware of these tensions, too.

Every leader and every member must come to grips with this reality. If you do, it will be the most freeing experience you will have in small group life. Master the fundamentals. But be prepared to manage the real tensions and challenges of everyday community. Very often you'll find there are no right answers to some problems that arise in small groups — just several good values and practices that you're trying to balance. Like walking a tightrope, balancing these tensions can be exhilarating and dynamic.

The Six Tensions

After evaluating the experiences and learning of several leaders, including our wives (who remain some of the best group leaders we know), we were able to identify at least six healthy tensions every small

The Six Challenges	The Six Tensions
The Learning Challenge	Truth . . . . .Life
The Development Challenge	Care . . . . .Discipleship
The Relational Challenge	Friendship . . . . . . .Accountability
The Reconciliation Challenge	Kindness . . . . .Confrontation
The Impact Challenge	Task . . . . .People
The Connection Challenge	Openness . . . . .Intimacy

group faces. The list is not exhaustive, and you may discover additional tensions along the way. But these six seem to capture much of what groups wrestle with while building community that transforms individuals and their world. So if you feel frustrated by a dilemma in your small group, perhaps we can relieve your stress. There may be no answer. It may be one of those "unsolvable problems" that place you squarely between two good things, and your job is not to find the answer but to manage the dynamic tension.

Walking the Small Group Tightrope will address these six challenges or tensions in the form of a continuum that represents the pull you feel when standing in the middle. Small group leaders reading this will gain skill in walking that tightrope. Small group members will learn to spot these tensions, adapt their perceptions and expectations of group life, and take next steps in building a community without compromise.

Every group faces these six tensions. Every group wants to create an environment in which people can learn about the faith, build truthful relationships, and grow spiritually. And every group must process disagreements and conflict, accomplish a mission, and help new people connect to the group. The six challenges are: a *learning* challenge, a *development* challenge, a *relational* challenge, a *reconciliation* challenge, an *impact* challenge, and a *connection* challenge.

Each challenge has an inherent tension. For example, the learning challenge requires a group to manage the truth-life tension. If you want people to learn truth, the truth of God's Word must connect with the story of their life. Too much story leaves no room for truth. Too much discussion of truth without connection to life can produce arrogant, puffed-up Christians who never practice what they study. We'll unpack this more later, but that gives you a sense of how we will approach the subject. Below are the six challenges and their associated tensions.

Small groups cannot thrive by focusing on either end of the continuum. They cannot choose friendship over accountability, kindness over confrontation, or task over community. Rather, effective life-giving small groups must embrace both ends of the continuum, in healthy opposition, and walk the tightrope between them toward authentic community and life change.

As we unpack these six areas your small group must manage, you'll come to a conclusion. If, in the end, you feel that small group leadership is like walking a tightrope, it means you get it.

In fact, some of the best small group leadership and participation happens on the tightrope. Each of the six areas we'll identify is a tightrope of its own, and the six taken together will keep you engaged in one of the most adventurous balancing acts of your life. As you embrace this fact and walk the tightrope, you will unleash latent energy in your group. No, it may not be easy. And it will require some work. But you are small group people, so you understand that.

Accordingly, this book contains eight chapters: this introduction, one chapter for each of the six challenges, and a conclusion. Each chapter will identify the challenge, define the inherent dynamics of the tension, describe what happens when groups lean too far toward one end of the continuum, and offer suggestions and tools so leaders can help their groups manage the polarities. After the conclusion, you'll find an appendix that includes a leader's guide for helping groups use this book with biblical material, group and personal assessments, and other exercises.

Remember, at each end of the continuum is something good, something that Scripture affirms and that groups must practice. So we'll spend time helping you understand each truth's biblical and practical implications. Then we'll explain that the tension point between the two is actually where groups find real progress and growth. Of course, the challenge for you as a leader is to help your group live there, so we'll offer helpful ideas, principles, and tools.

By the time you digest this content, you will understand how to meet these challenges by managing the tensions. The results will be life giving. Our exercises will help move your group forward in each area. And at the end of the book, we'll walk you through a summary exercise to help you formulate action steps to improve your small group's life and leadership.

By the time you complete your journey through the six healthy tensions, you will be ready to test them on your own and join the ever-adventurous, always-challenging experience of life in community. If we are right about these tensions, and this book helps you manage them more skillfully, perhaps your group will have a shot at knowing more of what Jesus prayed for when he asked the Father concerning us: "that they may be one as we are one" (John 17:11).

We have joined him in the dream that we can replicate on earth what he has known from eternity. Getting there will require walking a tightrope. So stretch those legs.

SIX WAYS TO IMPROVE YOUR BALANCE AS A GROUP LEADER

Leading a successful small group is like walking a tightrope. You traverse a taut, exciting line, balancing the dynamic tensions characteristic of every group. Drawing from the concept of "polarity management," Bill Donahue and Russ Robinson help you understand and deal with six dynamic areas every group leader must manage in order to create genuine, transforming small group community.

Your group is in for unprecedented connection and growth when you harness the interplay between

- Truth and Life
- Care and Discipleship
- Friendship and Accountability
- Kindness and Confrontation
- Task and People
- Openness and Intimacy

Effective, life-giving small groups learn how to embrace both ends of each continuum. *Walking the Small Group Tightrope* will strengthen your sense of balance, help you gain confidence as a leader, and show you how to release the untapped creative and relational energy in your group.

"Bless you—Bill and Russ—for telling it like it is as leaders of small groups. Your pain brought me hope—that God can use my mistakes. I wish this book had been around forty years ago when I started out. But for the next generation of leaders, it is going to make a BIG difference!" —Lyman Coleman, General Editor, *The Serendipity Bible*

Bill DONAHUE, Ph.D., *is executive director of Small Group Ministries for the Willow Creek Association. He has edited or contributed to many Willow Creek small group Bible study guides. He is the author of* Leading Life-Changing Small Groups *and coauthor of* The Seven Deadly Sins of Small Group Ministry.

Russ ROBINSON, J.D., *is senior pastor of Meadowbrook Church in North Haledon, New Jersey. Prior to that, he was director of ministries and small groups at Willow Creek Community Church. He is coauthor of* Building a Church of Small Groups.

CHURCH AND MINISTRY / MINISTRY RESOURCES / SMALL GROUP

US $12.99/UK £9.99/CAN $19.99
ISBN 0-310-25229-6

ZONDERVAN™

WWW.ZONDERVAN.COM

WILLOW CREEK RESOURCES

www.willowcreek.org

THE
SEVEN
DEADLY SINS OF
SMALL GROUP
MINISTRY

A TROUBLESHOOTING GUIDE FOR CHURCH LEADERS

BILL**DONAHUE**   RUSS**ROBINSON**

Sin One:
<u>Unclear Ministry Objectives</u>

Symptoms of Unclear Ministry Objectives

> *Leaders don't agree on the purpose for small groups*
> *The church's road to ministry progress is blocked*
> *Relationships are breaking down among those most committed to community*
> *Church members expect too much attention from the staff*
> *Small groups have a myopic vision and don't know their role in the overall church strategy*

It was the meeting to end all meetings. I (Bill) still get a shudder when I think of it. My son was in the Cub Scouts, and a meeting had been called for boys and their parents to attend. We arrived on time and took our place among the eleven boys and fifteen parents who were able to attend.

"Okay, so let's get started," began Kevin, the forty-five-year-old scoutmaster. "It is that time again when we should be thinking about the annual Cub Scout campout. Does anyone have any thoughts?"

"We will need some trucks to carry the garbage out after the boys leave," said one father.

"Why don't we have a different menu than last year?" asked Maria. "I think the boys are getting tired of peanut butter!"

About thirty seconds of silence reigned among us as we gathered in the cluttered church basement where these dreadful meetings were endured. Then seven-year-old Bobby broke the silence.

"What if it rains again? I hate it when it rains."

"You're a wimp!" said Mark, an eight-year-old veteran of camping life, whose speech was often laced with such encouraging words for his fellow Scouts. Others chimed in with their cracks and jokes.

"Okay, calm down. Let's just stay with the program we did last year," the scoutmaster suggested. "It seems like that worked fine."

Unless, that is, like our family, you were not involved last year. We had no idea what to expect this year or what had taken place last year as hundreds of young boys invaded the forests of Illinois.

"Last year was great . . ." started young Mike, pausing long enough for Kevin and the parents to think this whole camping experience might actually have some impact, ". . . if you like mosquitoes and mud!" The room erupted in laughter. Little Mike pleaded, "Please don't make us go to the same campground! That place was a swamp!" By now the boys were roaring hysterically and parents were needed to help restore order.

"That's enough boys—settle down. Parents, we need your help with this event. Who would like to volunteer to help this year?" asked Kevin. "We'll need about ten people. Our troop is responsible for organizing the sports equipment and games."

The response was unanimous: fifteen parents sat motionless as they pondered why they had chosen scouting instead of swimming lessons. *I could be lounging by the pool, getting a tan, watching my kids frolic in the warm summer sun. Instead I will probably be trudging through a sweltering forest, fending off insect attacks, and struggling to get three hours of sleep in a tent with a group of second graders whose life ambition is to do exactly the opposite of everything I say.*

"What about skills? Will the boys learn any skills?" asked Harold. At a Scout camp in 1967 Harold had learned to tie an assortment of knots. "I want my boy to learn something while he's there. Won't they learn to set up a tent, or carve something, or maybe build a fire?"

Harold's plea caught Kevin off guard. He was thinking logistics, not skills. He had parents to recruit, not kids to train.

Harold's comment forced me to think. *Isn't that what scouting is for? Isn't scouting supposed to train young men in the fine art of frontier survival—to impart skills for fending off wild animals without a weapon, catching fish with their bare hands, and building a log home without an axe? Scout camps should be raising up the next generation of Daniel Boones and Davy Crockets!*

"I don't want *my* son playing with fire," said Linda, who thinks the Cub Scouts are a babysitting service with uniforms. "The last thing I need is to spend all day in the emergency room! Oh, and my son Jimmy has a question. He wants to know if the kids will be allowed to bring video games along."

Sure. And why not a portable refrigerator, a mobile phone, and a laptop computer so he and the boys can keep up with the latest trends in the stock market? So much for developing the next King of the Wild Frontier.

"There will be plenty of safe things for the boys to do," assured a frustrated scoutmaster. "But no video games are allowed. Now, as I was saying, we will need people to plan the activities and supervise the boys at each of the sporting events. Does anyone have a bow and arrow and know how to shoot it?"

At this point in the meeting I wished I had brought one along. This misery had to end, one way or another. Others seemed to share this sentiment. (A few parents in the back of the room were contemplating a game of Russian roulette, several mothers were angry that their husbands were home watching baseball, and the boys—who had crossed the boredom threshold long ago—were beginning to plot the abduction of the scoutmaster one evening at camp.)

Mrs. Peters and her son Jeffrey, late arrivals to the meeting, suggested that all the parents attend the camp and share a tent so they could all "experience scouting firsthand." She was never seen again. Authorities are still looking for her. Well, actually that's not true, but it got pretty close.

"Why don't we just skip this year? Nobody has time to take three days off work in the middle of the week to help." A few others nodded.

"But then there would be no archery, BB guns, rope swings, or late-night campfire stories" lamented the boys.

And no mosquitoes, no portable toilets, and no muscle cramps, thought the parents.

By this point even our beloved scoutmaster had had about all he could take, so he raised his voice to get everyone's attention. "Look, we have to do this camp—all the other troops will be there, and it will be just fine! Now, who can help?"

Reluctantly parents began to volunteer, the boys agreed to quiet down long enough for some order to be maintained, and another summer scouting camp was on the calendar.

As I reflect on the experience, I realize it had all the makings of disaster from the start. In some general sense everyone knows that scouting is good for these boys and that camp is fun for them. But there was no clear vision for the event, no understanding of how it fit into the overall plan for developing these young kids, and no structure or process for getting to the desired outcomes. Every parent has a different definition of success for scouting and for the camp, so no consensus can be reached. People were frustrated and angry with the leader and with one another. Other than that, everything was just fine!

Small group ministries often suffer the same fate. There is a general sense that building community in the church is the right thing to do and that somehow small groups will help. But few understand or even agree on what must be done to get there. The leadership has failed to provide clarity—about God's call, the vision for their church, the purpose of groups, and the role each member plays in achieving the God-given vision. Other than that, every thing is just fine!

Why does this happen?

Because too many churches plunge into small group ministry without an end in mind. They're like the college kid who happily studies art and German poetry, works as a lifeguard each summer, then decides at graduation that he really wants to be a rocket scientist when he grows up. In church after church (Willow Creek included!), otherwise savvy adults begin building small groups without deciding what they want small group ministry to be "when it grows up."

In the excitement of starting groups, these churches might have great discussions about ministry models, group types, and spiritual formation objectives. But they never actually decide on the purpose of small groups or define how small groups will fit into church life. Inevitably these small group efforts reach an impasse. Church leaders who influence the congregation's strategic direction say the road to ministry progress seems blocked. Small group members, leaders, and coaches feel confused, angry, or indifferent about their groups' role in the church.

Lost in the Soup?

If the following case study sounds familiar, then your church probably suffers from unclear ministry objectives. We've changed the names, but here's what happened in a real meeting at a real church—a church that hasn't yet decided what it wants to be when it grows up. This church never really chose a small group ministry structure or analyzed the underlying values of different small group models.

Ten years ago this church started some groups, eventually assimilating about 30 percent of its adults into the groups. The board wants to grow the small groups ministry, so three months ago it unanimously approved a new small group model presented by Jennifer, the small groups pastor.

Jennifer now gives the board an enthusiastic update: "Things are going well. We have thirty-five groups, and I'm training coaches to oversee small group leaders. This will free me to develop and train more new leaders."

Suddenly Doug, a seasoned elder and board chairman, asks, "Bob, how's your class going? I see more people each Sunday. Does it use groups?" Jennifer pauses for Bob's response. Bob says the class doesn't use groups, but he loves teaching, and more members join each week. Doug says, "Classes are a great way to connect people that groups can't reach. We've had groups here for ten years, but many people haven't joined. We should beef up the classes."

Before Jennifer can jump in, Hank speaks. "What if we really promoted the classes? We have gifted teachers. Our service attendance is skyrocketing and we're bursting at the seams. If we don't get these people into a class or something soon, we'll lose them."

"Let's put that on the next agenda," Doug says. "Thanks, Jennifer, for spending a few minutes with us. You're doing fine work with small groups. Keep it up." Jennifer doesn't bow out yet, because she wants clarity. She says, "It was my understanding that our limited classroom facilities made small groups an imperative. We said that if we promote classes too much, we'll frustrate people." A few board members agree.

But then Mike says, "That's why we have to move even faster on the facilities options. Sarah, did you get that report on prospective sites?"

(Not privy to these discussions, Jennifer is surprised to learn that two weeks ago the board stepped up its land search.) Sarah, the building committee chairperson, says, "We've got some viable options. If people respond well, we could be in a new building in eighteen months!"

"Then we can really take a run at our space problem," Hank says. "Let's be sure to include six to ten new adult classrooms. That should accommodate the jump in attendance and help everyone find a place in the church. Let's take a look at possible locations right now."

Doug gracefully dismisses Jennifer. "Sorry, Jennifer, but we'll have to continue this discussion at another meeting. Now we need to jump on those potential properties, and it's confidential financial business. Thanks, again, for your input."

Jennifer leaves dejected. *Why build a group model,* she wonders, *that won't be supported or promoted? Why was the board so excited about groups three months ago but now appears ambivalent? Don't they see how groups and classes can work together to build community?*

When churches fail to choose a small group ministry model and define its underlying values, staff members become disillusioned, people remain unconnected, and the cause of Christ limps along instead of running at full throttle.

Small Group Models

Visionary leaders such as Ralph Neighbour, Carl George, Lyman Coleman, Roberta Hestenes, and Gareth Icenogle have provided great ideas for building transformational community through small groups. Together, their ideas comprise a continuum of small group models. Though each small group model is different, most fall into one of three categories along the continuum. We admit these categories risk over-simplification but believe they'll help you determine a direction and purpose for small groups in your church.

At one end of the continuum is the "church *with* small groups" category. In this model, small groups form a department, one of many in the church. At the continuum's other end is the "church *is* small groups" category. This model views each cell group as a little church. The "church *of* small groups" category views each group as a little community within the larger church. This church's staff and ministries are all built on a small groups skeleton, so that every member is connected through community to the church.

As we say repeatedly in public settings, Willow Creek Community Church has elected to be a church *of* small groups. But that model might not be best for your church. The deadly sin here isn't choosing a different model than we did. The sin is failing to wrestle this issue to the ground and make a clear statement of intent so that everyone in your church understands where small groups fit in your overall vision and strategy.

The telltale symptom of unclear ministry objectives is relationship breakdown among those people most committed to community. In the beginning everything is rosy. People discover a powerful vision for community—rooted in God's very nature. They see God using small groups to change lives. Leaders hone their leadership skills, shepherd people with intention, and develop the next generation of rising leaders. More people ask to get connected to groups.

But soon tough questions mount. "How do small groups work in the church? What happens to Sunday school? What are the implications for staff, volunteers, and current ministry initiatives?" As the church struggles to manage the tension, conflict rises. People ask why the senior pastor and board won't "get on board." Staff members wonder about their roles and job security and have trouble sustaining leaders and support systems. Meanwhile, senior leaders wonder why small groups won't get with the existing program. Some fear that renegade groups, flush with success, may spin off to form a new church.

It's ironic how much trouble could be avoided if churches first analyzed, then chose, from among the small group ministry models described in the following chart. We suggest you immerse yourself in the current literature about small groups. Remember, it's fine to pick and choose the values and strategies that best fit your ministry philosophy. You can use the chart to avoid mixing and matching incompatible components.

Small Group Models

	CHURCH WITH GROUPS	**CHURCH OF GROUPS**	**CHURCH IS GROUPS**
Purpose	Help People find a Place in the Church	A Means of Building the Church as Community	The Primary Expression of the Church
Organizing Principle	Someone Wants to Start a Group	Strategy using Affinity with Geography considered	Strategy using Geography with Affinity considered
Getting in a Group	Placement System (Centralized)	Group Invitation or Assimilation Event (Decentralized)	Assigned by Geography (Group responsible)
Group Membership	Optional for Growth Not Required for Church Membership	Essential for Growth Required for Church Membership	Essential for Growth Required for Church Membership
Role of Group Leaders	Mostly Reactive Leader	Proactive Shepherd-Leader	Pastoral Shepherd-Authority
Use of Curriculum	Chosen by Leader	Recommended by Staff or Chosen by Leader	Designated by Staff
Group Meeting Format	Designed by Leader or Curriculum	Designed by Leader + Ministry Strategy	Designed by Leader + Designated Pattern
Church Authority over Group	Low	Low	High
Church Monitoring of Groups	Low	High	High
Group-based Evangelistic Activity	Possible	Encouraged	Expected

197

Church with *Small Groups*

In the church *with* small groups model, everyone sees the purpose of small groups as one way for an interested person to connect with others. Other ministries are seen as equally valid ways to connect. Typical comments in such a church would be: "Hey, it's great you're in a group. Oh, you're in a class and not in a group? That's great too. Oh, you're on a committee, but you're not in a group or a class? That's great too." In other words, it's a choice, a way to connect. As long as you are connected somewhere, you're "in."

Turf wars are an inherent risk in churches *with* small groups, because the small group ministry competes with all other departments for leaders, financial support, meeting space, and visibility. Turf wars can get nasty every year at budget time: "How can you drop my guest speaker funding before you cut the brochure budget?" "Who needs a new church sign anyway?" "Let the youth bring their own furniture and food!"

Church of *Small Groups*

As you examine the chart of small group models, you could draw a heavy vertical line between the *church with* and *church of* models. Everything to the right of *church with* assumes that the whole church will be involved in groups. Crossing that line requires a total shift in church philosophy, the gravity of which must be weighed seriously.

The purpose of small groups in the *church of* model is to build the church as community. This model sees the larger community as a network of smaller communities that develop people in Christ. Therefore, the small groups concept penetrates every area of the church. Ministry leaders and congregation members become accustomed to designing and building ministry around a small group infrastructure. Small groups are not limited to any one department or subministry. But neither do they become the full expression of local church community life. In this philosophy you will hear neither "we have a small groups department" nor "the group is our church."

Church Is *Small Groups*

You will, however, hear "the group is our church" in the *church is* model. This model is obviously on the same continuum as *church of.*

But the *church is* model often differs in its theology of the nature and expression of church and in its intensity of small group emphasis.

The purpose for small groups in the *church is* paradigm is to be the church in its smallest form. This model sees small groups as the centerpiece of congregational life. Some advocates teach that "the church is the cell; the cell is the church." They emphasize that evangelism, worship, communion, and Bible study all take place in the group.

Let's face it. Regardless of the model you choose—*church with, of,* or *is*—your theology of the church will influence your decision. Some theologians believe a small group represents all the fullness of the bride of Christ. Others, however, would argue that small groups must be tied to a larger congregation for effective and accountable pastoral leadership, appropriate administration of the sacraments (even when observed at the small group level), sound biblical teaching, and church discipline.

Are Your Underlying Values Clear?

Churches that never commit to a ministry model lose the opportunity to define the underlying values of their small group ministry. Without defining your underlying values, how can you know what your small groups should accomplish or how they will change people?

At Willow Creek Community Church, we want to become a church *of* small groups. It is not a right or wrong decision. It is a clear decision. We all—from Senior Pastor Bill Hybels to elders, board, staff, and key volunteers—agreed on a dream to give every person that calls Willow Creek their church home a place in community. Small groups are central to our practice of community life and are our primary method for accomplishing ministry.

Beyond simply saying we want to give everyone a place in community, we decided to adopt—and adapt—the metachurch model developed by Carl George. The biblical theme underlying this model is its focus on enfolding the individual into community life, so each person is cared for and the community remains intact.

This theme surfaces in Exodus 18, when Jethro, Moses' father-in-law, observes that Israel, a complex nation, is not properly organized to adjudicate conflict among its members. Jethro prescribes guidelines for structuring the nation so all its people will be cared for but leaders won't burn out. (Don't you wish your father-in-law would do the same for your church?) Through his teaching ministry and writing, Carl George became a Jethro for us. He explained how Scripture—from Exodus 18 to Ezekiel 34 to Acts 6—shows God's concern that the individual never be overlooked within the larger community. God acts to ensure that people develop spiritually, resolve conflicts, have basic needs met, and are shepherded well by competent leaders.

Once we understood how these underlying biblical principles could be embodied in a ministry model, we shaped the way we organized small groups and modified the results we expect from them. Drawing on the examples of Jethro and Jesus, Carl George coined the term "span of care," which refers to the ability of one person to effectively respond to the needs of those they shepherd. Everyone should be cared for, but no one should be responsible for the care of too many. A reasonable span of care is that leaders should have no more than ten people in a group, and coaches should oversee only four or five leaders. Our coaches gather leaders in "huddles" to connect them for mutual learning and support. Coaches visit small groups to encourage leaders and groups as they build community together. And coaches meet one-on-one with small group leaders to develop and care for them. While these activities are never rigidly prescribed, they are practiced to ensure care for the flock.

Straining Gnats and Swallowing Camels

Over the last several months I (Russ) have visited several huddles and "superhuddles" (which include leaders, coaches, and staff leaders.) After numerous conversations with coaches, leaders, and apprentice leaders, a common theme emerged—too many people are not clear about our strategy. I thought, *This can't be! Didn't we already decide this?* After reflecting further, I realized that attaining clear ministry objectives requires more than a decision; it demands vigilance. We committed sin numero uno—again!

Two glaring symptoms led to our diagnosis that although our congregation has clearly embraced the goal of getting every member into a group, we've lost clarity about how groups fit into local church community life. One symptom is that many people are disappointed about not getting staff attention. They want Willow Creek Community Church to function like a traditional church, where they would call on the staff to address their needs. In turn, too many of us are being unduly responsive to those calls, so we lose the opportunity to have people cared for by their group or their small group leader. We are not honoring the strategy and structure we have put in place.

The second symptom of this ugly sin is that more and more people say, "I do groups, so I'm exempt from all other church activities, particularly evangelism." People have focused so intently on one part of our vision—groups—that they have missed the overall purpose of our church: to turn irreligious people into fully devoted followers of Christ. This comes dangerously close to pharisaic patterns of church life. And we cannot tolerate it.

The Pharisees became so focused on the system that they lost the big idea. They cleaned cups instead of hearts and followed the letter of the law but killed the spirit. As Jesus put it in Matthew 23:24, they strained gnats but swallowed camels. Our people have embraced group life, and have embraced it well. And we are thrilled. But some of them have contracted myopia and now see only the community, not those who stand outside it, far from God. If uncorrected, this nearsighted vision will result in "seeker blindness," the inability to see the plight of lost people. You likely have comparable issues to overcome as you dovetail small groups with other core objectives, whether evangelism, worship, or global ministry efforts.

At Willow Creek Community Church we're not just pursuing a metachurch model, we are also pursuing a seeker-targeted model. Jon Wallace, who led our small groups ministry from 1993 to 1995, once stated that Willow Creek was trying to do something unprecedented in church history. Willow Creek was pursuing a seeker-targeted, aggressively evangelistic weekend service model, while simultaneously pursuing the metachurch small group strategy, an aggressively community-oriented model. That combination has required intense effort and committed leadership every step of the way. (Which makes it clear why we have hit a few potholes on the implementation highway!)

Don't miss this issue. Whenever people grouse about your public services, evangelistic strategy, or any other central ministry philosophy, you have a clarity challenge. When you add small group issues to the mix, whether the metachurch model or another, you need even more ministry-level clarity on how small groups fit into the church. The two root causes of this confusion are fuzzy churchwide goals and ministry nonalignment.

Fuzzy Churchwide Goals

I (Bill) recently flew to Europe to teach on behalf of the Willow Creek Association, a worldwide network of over seven thousand local churches with similar values. While I waited for a plane from Frankfurt to Geneva, the loudspeaker said: "Mr. Sagamoto, please report to gate B24 immediately. Flight 1135 is waiting. Mr. Sagamoto, please report to the gate." Ten minutes later the message came again. Then again.

My guess is that flight 1135 had 238 passengers on the list and 237 of them were getting angry. I pictured Mr. Sagamoto sitting in an airport lounge, sound asleep from the jet lag after a fifteen-hour flight. "Your flight is waiting. Please report to the gate!" Even the announcer sounded peeved. By then, if I were Mr. Sagamoto, I might have decided to take another flight, if only to avoid 237 angry passengers. I'd imagine my picture and story on the news: "Transatlantic flight delayed by sleeping passenger. Passengers miss connecting flights all over Europe. Economy suffers setback. Sagamoto beaten with pillows and blankets while boarding. Remains in critical condition."

Some churches are stuck at the small group departure gate because someone is not on board and refuses to fly. It may be the pastor, a key elder, or a staff member. Or it may be that everyone agrees flying is the right thing to do; they just all want different planes and schedules. A stuck church have worked through the *church with-of-is* issue to gain consensus on how they want to live out community. They've selected a model and adapted it to their context, creating a "when our small groups grow up" goal. Yet they can't get the plane off the ground, because it's not enough to create conceptual clarity about direction and design. You must also translate these concepts for every ministry setting where you expect small groups to take root. All the ministries must get on board for this flight to take off. Simply agreeing to the process (flying) and objective (Paris) is not enough. We must fly the same plane together and arrive as a community.

At Willow Creek we've agreed on a churchwide set of terms to clearly embed goals in every ministry setting. We've expressed our small group goals through both quantitative and qualitative statements.

The Five Gs: Our Term for Individual and Organizational Goals

We use "the five Gs" as a framework for individual spiritual development. For example, when a person becomes an official member, we ask them questions in each area.

- *Grace.* How does someone become a Christian in the true sense of the word? How did that happen for you?

- *Growth.* How are you presently nurturing your spiritual growth through spiritual disciplines on your own?

- *Group.* Are you connected to a small group of believers here at Willow Creek for the purpose of growth, loving support, and accountability?

- *Gifts.* Are you responsibly using your spiritual gifts in a place of service within the church?

- *Good Stewardship.* In light of the tithe as a biblical precedent for giving, do you regularly support this body, using 10 percent as a goal to reach (or surpass as God prospers)?

This common terminology for goals helps individuals affirm their commitment to Christ and this church, as well as assess their next steps for spiritual growth. We form our small group curricula around the five Gs, so small group leaders use the same ideas and language in their groups as we do in the church. We also apply the five Gs to organizational goals. Regarding our goal to grow in grace, we talk about individuals experiencing and extending grace, and we also describe how we think God wants to build Willow Creek as a grace-filled community.

Qualitative and Quantitative Goals

At Willow Creek we get a lot more specific than simply saying we want to become a church *of* small groups. We clarify our churchwide and ministry-level objectives by making *qualitative* and *quantitative* statements about small groups. Setting and reaching such goals is a challenge. For example, in 1995 we set a goal to "give everyone who calls Willow Creek their church home a place in community." Try that in a church where weekend attendance exceeds 17,000.

We qualitatively defined "a place in community." It meant that every person needed to be connected to a group with an identified, qualified leader. We wanted every person in every group (beginning at age three in Promiseland, our children's ministry) to view their group as their primary community. This implied that every group needed to become a community of care for each individual. And it required quality leaders who would do their best to nurture each person along spiritually.

Regarding quantity, we wanted it to become abnormal for a person not to be in a group. When a person showed up at Willow Creek and was asked, "What small group are you in?" and they answered, "I'm not in one," there would be shock and dismay, because it would be viewed as abnormal to be disconnected from the community.

We went so far as to put a number and timeline to this goal. For example, in 1995 we had approximately 8,000 people in small groups, so we thought we could connect 20,000 people in small groups by the end of the year 2000.

Clear whole-church objectives, fleshed out in the form of goals, forced us to draw a line in the sand. It was a declaration that Willow Creek Community Church would become a different kind of church in five years, as God worked among us. It would become our expression of the body of Christ, working together for his purposes, in South Barrington, Illinois, for the next five years.

We still needed to give each leader a part to play in achieving the dream. Having declared what the future might look like if God so blessed, we broke the churchwide goal into pieces so that those in each ministry— couples, singles, men, women, students, children, seekers, the hurting, and volunteers—could share in the objective. It made our dream tangible. Every ministry had a commitment to a clear ministry objective.

Ministries out of Alignment

Besides setting clear churchwide goals, we also needed to align our ministries, both vertically (with the church's mission) and horizontally (with one another). Churches with ministry-level nonalignment will not bridge the gap between clear objectives and the realization of their dream for community.

Setting goals and then breaking them down to a departmental level leads to interesting conversations, because people have to start pursuing the church's agenda and not simply their own. These conversations have brought out the best from our leaders. From musicians to women's leaders, from care-based ministries and men's ministry to single adults and students, we have come together to try to build a church *together*. It forces alignment.

Vertical alignment means matching leadership objectives with leadership practice. It declares, "Our church knows our direction. We prayed it through, listened to wise counsel, and have come to consensus among our senior leaders. We've specified it, described it, and diagrammed it. We have paid attention to quality and quantity outputs for each ministry and the church as a whole. Now, everybody, let's get together and work toward that goal."

Horizontal alignment gets everyone in sync as they move toward the vertical, or overall, churchwide goal. Horizontal alignment requires moving ministry leaders beyond simply communicating with each other, toward coordinating and collaborating with each other. At first, ministries moving toward vertical goals are like a marching band with great music but no sense of formation or cadence. They step on each other's toes and bungle opportunities. Later they learn to address opportunities together.

For example, our Promiseland ministry presents wonderful opportunities for horizontal ministry alignment, because so many children visit our campus each year. Their parents may not want to attend church yet and may simply drop off their older kids or send their children with another family. They may think, *Church is good for my kids, but not for me yet.*

Remember the pharisaical problem we described in groups that have tunnel vision and are losing sight of seekers? They've embraced the Group G goal for individuals within their small groups, but they've forgotten that Willow Creek promotes community for a cause. If, however, we encourage key groups to realign horizontally, imagine the possibilities. They can capitalize on the Promiseland opportunity. Our couples' ministry, men's ministry, and women's ministry can probably work through those Promiseland children to reach their not-yet-attending parents. We just need to sit down together and dream.

How clear have you been with each ministry about your objectives as a church? Have you created qualitative and quantitative goals for becoming a church of small groups, having people realize the Group G in their daily experience as Christ followers? Is everyone clear about his or her part of the mission? Does everyone understand how their small group aligns with other groups in fulfilling the whole-church mission?

Graduate-Level Clarity

Forming a clear purpose for your church and its small group direction and carrying it out throughout the church requires a graduate school work ethic. Once the sin of unclear ministry objectives is exposed and confessed, the real labor begins. But here's the good news. When you determine your small groups direction, express that in a well-formulated model, and then align yourselves around specific goals, you'll feel remarkable energy. While we at Willow Creek still commit our fair share of sin in this area, our hard work has paid off. We now have several thousand leaders moving us in the same direction.

The next chapter will describe strategies and tools that helped us along the way. We hope that as you use them or adapt them, you will gain clarity about where you are headed and how to get there with integrity and focus.

We might wonder what would have happened in Jennifer's life had the meeting described earlier in this chapter taken a different turn. What if the church had really known what it was called to become, had worked to clarify a strategy and model, had adapted the core components of that model to its setting and culture, and had then aligned the ministries around achieving that aim? She would have finished her presentation and the board would have had increased confidence in her leadership.

Jennifer would probably be back in her office taking the next step in the small group process. She'd be putting together strategies and tools so leaders could implement what the elders, board, and staff had so wholeheartedly committed to. And her task, despite its challenges and occasional heartbreaks, would allow her to travel to challenging ministry destinations instead of staying stuck, idling at the gate. *Please stand by while we try to get you an update on the delayed departure of flight 1135.* No thanks. We're changing airlines.

NOW
that you've put your small groups together,

how do you keep them from falling apart?

Lots of books have been written on how to put a

small group ministry together. Here's how to keep yours running.

The Seven Deadly Sins of Small Group Ministry is your manual

for troubleshooting the sticking points that can hinder the small

groups ministry in your church. This practical, solutions-focused

book is like no other. Put it in your library today. You'll be

sure to reach for it tomorrow.

Cover design: Holli Leegwater

CHURCH AND MINISTRY / MINISTRY RESOURCES / SMALL GROUP

WWW.ZONDERVAN.COM

US $19.99/ $29.99 CAN

ISBN 0-310-24706-3

51999

9 780310 247067

EAN

BUILDING A CHURCH
OF SMALL GROUPS

a place
where
nobody
stands
alone

BILLDONAHUE RUSS**ROBINSON**

FOREWORD BY JOHN ORTBERG

In the Beginning, God:
The Theological Evidence

Whatever community exists as a result of God's creation, it is only a reflection of an eternal reality that is intrinsic to the being of God. Because God is eternally one, when he created in his image, he created oneness.

GILBERT BILEZIKIAN, COMMUNITY 101

"Ladies and gentlemen of the jury. Yours is an awesome responsibility. Soon we will conclude our closing arguments, and you will render the verdict. Our society trusts fallible men and women with decisions like the ones you now face. Soberly and objectively, you must review the evidence. Our arguments are not evidence; you must judge our closing statement to determine how you view the evidence. The verdict will rest with you. But we believe there is clear and convincing proof for building a church of small groups. We'll begin by reviewing the theological evidence for community."

The arguments from theology—that is, the study of God and his person—prove beyond doubt that God's nature is communal. Our theological analysis will show you why God's communal nature requires you to respond by building community—for yourself and for your church.

The theological case depends on three basic ideas. First, God exists in community; he has forever existed as and will into eternity remain three persons in One. Second, God was incarnate in Christ Jesus, whose transformational relationships offer a model you cannot ignore. Third, Jesus dreams of oneness for all Christians, which is why you must move your church toward his vision.

The God of Community

You've read Genesis 1:26: "Then God said, 'Let us make man in our image, in our likeness....'" But have you noticed its remarkable expressions of plurality? These thirteen words include three references to God's unique nature. Note the references to "us" and "our," which proclaim the core doctrine of the Trinity. At the same time, God's singularity is a core doctrine of the church universal. As Deuteronomy 6:4 says, "Hear, O Israel: The LORD our God, the LORD is one." In other words, God begins Scripture and the creation story with the theological idea of plurality within oneness.

The creation account provides us an amazing window into the nature of the community of God, in whose image we are created. This plurality of beings comes to consensus to create humans in their image. They create in their collective image, which, in part, is a community-bearing image. It is not enough to say God is interested in community or even obsessed with community. God, rightly defined and understood, *is* community.

The doctrine of the Trinity is complex. Orthodox Christians have for generations accepted that God is Three in One, but few of us think much about it. This seemingly enigmatic doctrine of the Trinity, however, has massive implications. As Gareth Icenogle explains:

> The small group is a generic form of human community that is trans-cultural, trans-generational and even transcendant. The call to human gathering in groups is a God-created (ontological) and God-directed (theological) ministry, birthed out of the very nature and purpose of God's being. God as Being exists in community. The natural and simple demonstration of God's communal image for humanity is the gathering of the small group.[1]

Did you catch that? "God's communal image for humanity is the gathering of the small group." The entire Bible proclaims that God (expressed singularly) exists from all time and for all time in community as the Trinity (plurality). This Trinitarian doctrine begins with the creation account, where all three persons of the Trinity are present. When God created the world, "the Spirit of God was hovering over the waters" (Genesis 1:2). John describes Jesus as the agent of Creation: "In the beginning was the Word, and the Word was with God.... Through him all things were made; without him nothing was made that has been made" (John

1:1–3). Since God himself lives and works in community and since we are created in God's image, then we too are created in and for community.

You cannot come to understand the true nature of God unless and until you accept that he is not simply an individual. God is, in every sense of the word, a "group" as well. In the biblical framework (see, for example, Matthew 18:15–20), whenever "two or three come together" in God's name, they together have an ability to act in concert for the good of themselves and others. Something unique happens when individuals work together. So it is with God in the Trinity. Without an ounce of sacrilege, we might call the Godhead the first small group!

I (Bill) never fully understood this until I heard Dr. Gilbert Bilezikian first preach on community. He was one of the first theologians to present not only the powerful triune nature of God but also the relational aspects. If you want a vision for the kind of community that Gilbert shared with us, then read *Community 101*. Gilbert describes the community as both vertical and horizontal—just like the bars on a cross. They meet in the center, and true community is born when we experience God and all of his fullness and his people in all of their fullness.

In God there is the identity of the One, and yet there are Three in One. There is distinctive individuality. God exists in community. This picture of the oneness of God shatters our independence.

The Community Gene

Let's dig deeper into the statement "Let *us* make man in *our* image." What are the implications of being image bearers, ones who bear a likeness to this community defining God?

It is clear what this does not mean. We are not triune deities. (Only a schizoid person says, "I am God, and so am I"!) So we know our image bearing must mean something other than a direct, one-to-one correlation of God's community likeness.

Some might suggest that while God is indeed three persons in One, bearing his image refers to having eternal souls, as distinct from the rest of the creation. That seems an unlikely understanding. If the intent of the passage was to distinguish humans from the rest of creation, the statement among the persons of the Trinity might be more like this: "Let us make man unlike any other creation so far. Let us give him a distinctive spiritual dimension and existence, so humans are unique among the created." But that is not what God says.

In constructing humans, God trumped all his design work. He performed a kind of crowning creative act we don't often grasp. Sure, he gave humans a soul dimension, a spiritual existence that distinguishes us from plants, animals, and other created elements. Then he did more—much, much more. God chose to embed in us a distinct kind of relational DNA. God created us all with a "community gene," an inborn, intentional, inescapable part of what it means to be human.

This "relational DNA" or "community gene" helps explain why churches need small groups. People don't come to church simply to satisfy spiritual needs. They come to us internally wired with a desire for connection. They see church as a likely place to discover God's involvement in creation and in their lives. Their hunger for togetherness is an inescapable mark of humanity. If we treat this hunger casually, we subtly deny the truth of creation. However, when our churches own the responsibility to move people into relationship, we validate the nature of the God whose image we bear. We are created in God's image; therefore, we are created for community. It's part of being an image bearer of God himself.

Community Transcends Culture

You don't have to be a Christian or churchgoer to understand that people need each other. Prisoners know the pain of being behind bars, away from the community of normal life. They view "solitary confinement" as even worse. Being subjected to extended aloneness kills the spirit, introduces insanity, and destroys a person.

Senator and former Vietnam POW John McCain describes the elation he experienced when he was reunited with fellow prisoners after a horribly long and brutal separation:

> I was overwhelmed by the compulsion to talk nonstop, face-to-face with my obliging new cellmate. I ran my mouth ceaselessly for four days. . . . One of the more amusing spectacles in prison is the sight of two men, both just released from solitary, talking their heads off simultaneously, neither one listening to the other, both absolutely enraptured by the sound of their voices.[2]

We all know the differences between introverts and extroverts. Some of us seek more solitude than others do. Yet, we also know that even introverts need the companionship of other people, because, more than any other creatures, humans are ravenously relational. We seek each other out. We meet, court, and marry. We define life by the community of family. We prize functional families and friends, relationships that are loyal and true, safe and loving. Only the sociopath (defined as one departed from the norm) ultimately rejects relationship. The rest of us—regardless of age, gender, race, temperament, or past history—realize that part of being human means having an insatiable hunger for community.

Paul, apostle to the Gentiles, explains why every society recognizes this human passion for connection. "From the time the world was created, people have seen the earth and sky and all that God made. They can clearly see his invisible qualities—his eternal power and divine nature. So they have no excuse whatsoever for not knowing God" (Romans 1:20 NLT). Since part of that "divine nature" is the plurality of God and his own craving for community, God's created testimony makes it plain to unbelievers that people need each other.

Believers understand that everyone hungers for community, first, because of who God is, and further, because we bear God's communal image. Dallas Willard explains how understanding the doctrine of the Trinity should change our lives:

> . . .nearly every professing Christian has some information about the Trinity, the incarnation, the atonement, and other standard doctrines. But to have the "right" answers about the Trinity, for example, and to actually *believe* in the reality of the Trinity, is all the difference in the world.
>
> The advantage of believing in the reality of the Trinity is not that we get an A from God for giving "the right answer." Remember, to believe something is to act as if it is so. . .the advantage of *believing* in the Trinity is that we then live as if the Trinity is real: as if the cosmos environing us actually is, beyond all else, a self-sufficing community of unspeakably magnificent personal beings of boundless love, knowledge, and power. And, thus believing, our lives naturally integrate themselves, through our actions, into the reality of such a universe, just as with two plus two equals four.[3]

Let's now sum up the first evidence in the theological case for community. God is three and yet One. We are created in God's community-bearing image. Both the Bible and the creation teach us that to be human is to hunger for community. Therefore, if we compromise community within the church, we compromise our essence as created persons.

Jesus in Community

The second piece of evidence in the theological case for community flows from God's actual entrance into human history. In our own lives we meet God incarnate, that is, God becoming flesh, the "God with us," the Immanuel, Jesus Christ.

Through their accounts of Christ's conduct, the Gospels reveal what it means to bear the created image of the triune God. Jesus' entire public ministry models what it means to live in community. His pattern shows us why community—most particularly, community experienced through small group relationships—is a necessity, not an option, for those of us who bear his name.

You can see the drama of Jesus' relational choices in the third chapter of Mark. Early in his ministry, he drew crowds wherever he went. People heard about the power of his words and deeds, and, as Mark describes, they chased him:

> Jesus withdrew with his disciples to the lake, and a large crowd from Galilee followed. When they heard all he was doing, many people came to him from Judea, Jerusalem, Idumea, and the regions across the Jordan and around Tyre and Sidon. Because of the crowd he told his disciples to have a small boat ready for him, to keep the people from crowding him. For he had healed many, so that those with diseases were pushing forward to touch him. (Mark 3:7–10)

Some of us might seize such a moment to leverage the crowd. Interpreting the large audience as a sure sign of God's presence and anointing, we might try to attract more audience share, step up publicity, explore logistics for handling larger crowds, and propose a building project.

Not Jesus. He did not equate plenty of people with true community. In fact, instead of working the crowd, he muffled it and pulled away. "Jesus went up on a mountainside and called to him those he wanted" (Mark 3:13). Jesus invited twelve men to join him in a three-year, life-transforming, ministry-embedding journey.

His connection with the disciples is a perfect example of relational interdependence. Jesus knew the masses had deep needs. Yet, he spent most of his public ministry doing life and ministry together with his little community of twelve disciples. He drew away from the many, then selected a few to reach the many. As Eugene Peterson explains, "Jesus invested 90 percent of his time with twelve Jewish men so that he could reach all Americans."[4]

215

Jesus followed the divine pattern of gathering a few so that he would transform many lives. Jesus has existed from all time in the community of Three in One, the gathering of few. It was inevitable—because of his nature and identity—that when Jesus became incarnate as a human being, like us bearing the created image of the triune God, he gathered a few into community.

Lone Rangers Are Alone Rangers

We've examined two pieces of evidence for community. As created beings we were formed for community. As Christ-followers we are transformed for community. Nevertheless, because our culture emphasizes individualism and self-reliance, many Christians miss the testimony of Christ's life. They think they can be Christlike without pursuing community life.

Many of us in the church view community as optional. As Willow Creek's Director of Small Groups, I (Russ) talk with veteran Christians who resist being connected into what they call "the system." Both long-term "Creekers" and churched people who have moved here decline formal connection to the church or a small group. We lovingly call them "renegades."

Some of them are "church-hopping renegades." Applying consumerism philosophy to their church engagement, they treat Willow Creek like one item on a Chicagoland church buffet. Their agenda is to get themselves and their family "fed,"[5] the tastiness of the entrée the sole measure of whether they will grace our establishment again. Life-transforming community is not part of the nutrition plan.

Granted, the church has done them few favors. We paint a picture of Christianity rightly lived as a simple matter of you and your relationship with God. Such minimalist, "fire insurance" versions of faith may escape hell. But they have nothing to do with following Jesus. Following Jesus means following him into community.

Some people go a little further than an "independent contractor" mindset toward God—to a cheapened version of community sometimes labeled "fellowship." We grew up in several different churches and denominations, all of which fed us fellowship dinners in the fellowship hall during fellowship gatherings. Call it "community lite." While our upbringing provided many good gifts, our malnourished communities dramatically undersold the kind of oneness inherent in the Trinity and modeled by Christ's life.

I (Bill) experienced this starvation diet early in my Christian life. Having come to faith in a church that had no groups, I was eager for community and soon found it in a small group of friends. They had begun a home Bible study to nourish believers and reach seekers. We began to invite lost friends. Soon our Bible study grew to thirty-five people, half of whom did not know Christ. Our experience was unbelievable. Lives were changing, believers were encouraged, and the lost were seeing firsthand what true spiritual community can look like. Then the church shut us down. They worried that too many "publicans and sinners" at church might sway our young people. They feared that our new believers would become like the sinners. It never occurred to them that the reverse might happen. Once again, true community was shelved.

Of course, sometimes we stumbled into deeper Christian friendships, rare and wonderful clues of our God-designed bent toward connection. Sometimes our families gave us a taste of this community. We wondered whether parachurch organizations offered what we sought. Painful as it is to admit, somewhere along the way, the dozen or so otherwise decent churches of which we were a part lost the biblical concept of community as God designed it and as Jesus showed us.

Many churches today lack intentional community life. We love Willow Creek Community Church, but it has sometimes fallen far short of the ideal expressed in a most basic theology. During exponential growth, authentic connection at Willow Creek has at times been the exception rather than the rule. We have far to go before the majority experience what the disciples tasted in Christ's company. It is a huge task to connect a whole church full of people, let alone have them experience community like Jesus knows and models it.

But the evidence from Jesus' life compels us to stay the course, to resist resistance. When the church renders its verdict on Jesus in community, it must remodel its foundation according to Christ's example of group life.

Discipleship Is about Oneness

There is some consolation in knowing that even Jesus, after a three-year investment in twelve disciples, fell short of what he knew was possible for their community. The way he expressed the shortcoming provides the third piece of evidence in the theological case for small groups.

We find this evidence in John's account of the end of Jesus' ministry. In John 17, Jesus offers an awe-inspiring glimpse of God's ideal for his children: that they live in oneness. The Trinitarian and incarnational evidence is strong; John 17, however, may be the defining piece of evidence in the theological case for small groups. Every lawyer dreams of finding a smoking gun, the surefire proof in a case. If ever there was a smoking gun on community, it is John 17.

Notice the chapter's setting. Jesus is having a final, pre-death, extended conversation with his heavenly Father. The eleven remaining disciples are still gathered around Jesus despite the dismissal of Judas and their own infighting for prominence. They hang on Jesus' every word, having been humbled by slavish foot-washing. We are not sure where they are, whether still at the table or in the Garden of Gethsemane, but Jesus prays to his Father while his friends wait.

This poignant passage gives us an insiders' look at Jesus' prayer. Jesus prays as One who, from and for all time, shares essence of being with God, talking to another with whom he has existed in the most intimate of relationships.

Another factor is at play in this conversation. It is sometimes said that when someone faces death, one's conversation reveals his or her deepest passions, hopes, and dreams. That's why we go out of our way to honor dying wishes. In his final hours, Jesus gives us clues to his chief concerns.

Jesus knows that in a few hours he will become God's ultimate sacrificial lamb. Death is a certainty, save a last-minute move by God to change salvation history. While conversing with his heavenly Father, Jesus speaks penetrating words that show the magnificence he accords this thing we call community. He prays for the band of followers he has gathered, particularly for the disciples with whom he spent the most time modeling community. "I will remain in the world no longer, but they are still in the world, and I am coming to you. Holy Father, protect them by the power of your name—the name you gave me—so that they may be one as we are one" (John 17:11).

"So that they may be one as we are one." If you have any theological sense of what Jesus is saying, you recognize that statement's overwhelming punch. Jesus says, "I want human beings—for example, these men into whom I've poured my life—to find the kind of oneness we experience in the Trinity." The Triune community that is the first community. The Godhead that is the model community. Jesus really thinks this is possible!

What do you do with these words? Note how well Jesus' final conversation with his Father applies to small group ministry, to building community within a local church. Jesus chose a particular way to invest three years of his life in public ministry. He has rallied others to himself, poured his life into them, and now trusts them to extend his people-investment strategy and ministry. On his final night, he asks his heavenly Father for something specific—to grant his community the gift of oneness.

Imagine if Jesus had taken prayer requests from his disciples. Earlier they had asked for positions of honor to the exclusion of others—right-hand man status—or assurances of future security for having thrown in their lot with Jesus. "Overthrow Rome!" they might plead. Some would settle for good fishing weather; others would want the promise of future ministry on the same terms as they had known it. Community? Not in a million years!

But that is what Jesus asks of God. He asks for them to know oneness. Not just any kind of oneness, however. No, Jesus is much more bold. He asks for his followers to experience an incredible payoff in community. He requests no less than Trinity-level relationship!

When I (Russ) first was gripped with the nature of Jesus' prayer, I was forever changed. I had started exploring a move from practicing law to vocational ministry, because Senior Pastor Bill Hybels had invited me to become Willow Creek's director of small groups. Aside from the complications of such a transition, I was reluctant to turn over my life for something that held mere strategic leadership interest. I had been a Willow Creek elder long enough to see the impact of our transition to becoming a church of small groups. I could see that a small group foundation made sense in terms of good managerial practice. But I had never grappled with the deeper issues. Some elder, huh?

I began realizing that, unless I was fueled by a passion for community that transcended a wise church program, I could never leave my law practice. I prayed for God to endow me with a larger vision for small groups. Then I waited. No books helped me. Conversations with small groups gurus did little. One sleepless night, I sat in a Denny's restaurant (the only place open at 2:00 a.m. to tortured souls), and reread John 17. God answered my prayer with these words from the lips of Jesus: "So that they may be one as we are one."

These verses overwhelmed me with the implications for small group ministry. Jesus actually prayed that real people—this little band of real, live flawed followers—would find an amazing kind of oneness. That it's even possible for humans to find such relational connection is remarkable. Yet Jesus says it is available. You can request it!

Even more stunning, Jesus doesn't stop by requesting oneness for his inner circle. He shifts his focus to a broader audience: "My prayer is not for them alone. I pray also for those who will believe in me through their message, that all of them may be one, Father, just as you are in me and I am in you" (John 17:20–21). Jesus, on death row for our redemption, prayed a real prayer at a real place at a real time, not just for his followers, but for you, each person you know, each Christ-follower you are acquainted with in your church, every human being to believe in him. He prayed a prayer that they would find that same kind of oneness that he wanted for his followers, oneness that matched his experience in the Trinity.

Decision Time

Now, *you* have to do something with that prayer. You can conclude that those were just flowery words, or that Jesus was in an emotional panic and didn't know what he was saying, but you have to do something with them. Can we conclude that he really meant what he prayed?

I did—so much so that I knew my best efforts and gifts would have to be put against the task of building a church of small groups, no matter what. I purposed that, until God clearly called otherwise, I had to be in on this mission. Ultimately it meant the sale of a law firm partnership, a move from the marketplace to vocational ministry, and a relearning of all new occupational skills. But I had to do something with the echo of Jesus' prayer and its implications for my church.

What does your church do with those words? Christ prayed for oneness among his immediate followers and those who would believe later. Is that the routine experience of your church? Probably not. Somehow churches have lost this vision. A cheapened theology has led to a cheapened doctrine of the church, a two-bit theology of community. Churches respond to Jesus' call with bargain-basement fellowship. We cannot settle for anything less than Jesus' dream of community. New visions, strategies, and tactics worthy of the theological model of oneness—these are not optional!

What if Jesus is describing a relational connection among mortal men and women that can only be explained theologically? The church can then join him in a grand vision of Christian friendship, unique from anything society can offer. We can refine our theology and be formed by our doctrine of God and the Trinity. The path to community is bound up in the person and identity of God himself.

Gilbert Bilezikian—one of Willow Creek's founders, Wheaton College professor emeritus, and our mentor on community—explains why the theological case for community is so important.

> This concern for the survival of the church down through the ages provides the explanation for the anguished tones of Jesus' prayer. He knew that if the church should fail to demonstrate community to the world, it would fail to accomplish its mission, because the world would have reason to disbelieve the gospel (vv. 21, 23). According to that prayer, the most convincing proof of the truth of the gospel is the perceptible oneness of his followers.[6]

In other words, only by understanding God's identity and nature can we experience the oneness he desires for his followers. God existed from and for all time, in and as community. God incarnate, by image and identity, led a life and ministry of radical relationship. Jesus knew, in fact, that only one standard could express the kind of friendship his followers should find in the community of faith—the standard of God's relational identity and Trinitarian nature.

If you allow yourself to embrace the full implications of Jesus' dream for community, it will grip your heart. It will motivate you to say, "I don't know what it's going to take to make that happen within a local church, but whatever it's going to take, we're going to wrestle through and figure it out." We have to rebuild biblical, theologically sound community as best we can. We must study, think, and plan ways for people to become spiritually mature through transformational relationships. Maybe, just maybe, real people in our day will begin to experience the kind of oneness God dreams they will find.

This is what God dreams for us and our churches. We are called to move into community, one at a time, on the basis of God's identity as Three in One. We cannot ignore his example in Christ's incarnation and parting prayer; these call every church to weave real community into the fabric of its life. We must find ways to answer that call by creating an expanding network of small groups. That is the theological case. The evidence is overwhelming. But it is just the beginning.

"The single most helpful resource on small groups I've read. Combines experience-based practicality with biblically rooted wisdom to encourage soul connecting."

LARRY CRABB / Psychologist, Author, and Founder of New Way Ministries

"*Building a Church of Small Groups* is not a theoretical book or one written by someone with a year's experience. Donahue and Robinson have done what they write about. Not just once, but many times. And they have proved their principles in one of the greatest churches in the world. Every page drips with the integrity of something tried and proven to be workable. This one's a 'church-changer.'"

GORDON MACDONALD / Author, *Ordering Your Private World*

"Bill Donahue and Russ Robinson have not just thought and read and talked about community. They have rolled up their sleeves and devoted their vocational lives to figuring out how to actually help make it happen with real-life people in a real-life church."

JOHN ORTBERG / Author, *If You Want to Walk on Water, You've Got to Get Out of the Boat*

CHURCH SHOULD BE THE LAST PLACE WHERE ANYONE STANDS ALONE

"Building a church of small groups, not just a church with small groups, takes vision and some serious how-to. Bill Donahue and Russ Robinson have given us both."

RANDY FRAZEE / Author, *The Connecting Church*

"Donahue and Robinson have developed a complete yet concise framework for structuring a practical and holistic church-wide small group ministry. This book is personal, accessible, and vulnerable. It is in touch with the hard realities of what it takes to partner with God's Spirit to bring about positive change for a postmodern church."

GARETH W. ICENOGLE / Author, *Biblical Foundations for Small Group Ministry*

Cover design: Jamie K. DeBruyn
Cover photos: FPG / PhotoDisc / Digital Vision / Photonica

CHURCH & MINISTRY / MINISTRY RESOURCES / SMALL GROUP

WILLOW CREEK RESOURCES.

www.willowcreek.com

US $19.99/$29.95 CAN
ISBN 0-310-24035-2

ZONDERVAN™

WWW.ZONDERVAN.COM

The Connecting Church

BEYOND SMALL GROUPS TO
AUTHENTIC COMMUNITY

Church

RANDY FRAZEE

FOREWORDS BY

LARRY CRABB • GEORGE GALLUP JR. • DALLAS WILLARD

THE LONELIEST NATION ON EARTH

To all appearances and by all standards the Johnsons have a wonderful life. They own a house in a nice suburb with four bedrooms, two baths, and a rear entry two-car garage. Their house is surrounded by a six-foot fence to provide privacy for an in-ground pool, barbecue grill, and patio furniture. Bob and Karen have two children—a boy and a girl. Each of them has a college degree; they both work and have a combined household income well above the average for their community. Most important, everyone in the family is in good health.

Yet if you could enter the hearts and thoughts of Bob and Karen Johnson, you would discover that they have dreams and fears no one else knows about. While they have never voiced it to anyone, there is an increasing sense of isolation, distress, and powerlessness growing inside of them. In a nutshell, the Johnsons have done a fine job "keeping up with the Joneses," but they still are not happy.

How could this be? The Johnsons are living the American Dream. There are so many people who are less fortunate. Actually, this personal dilemma, which is quietly gnawing away a sense of contentment in the Johnsons, is a national epidemic—and their experience is no surprise to sociologists and pollsters. George Gallup Jr. concluded from his studies and polls that Americans are among the loneliest people in the world.[1] This seems unbelievable when you think of the availability of transportation and the billions of dollars of discretionary money available for entertainment. Americans can buy so much activity—how can they possibly be so lonely? Today more than three-fourths of the American people live in metropolitan areas, and more than two-thirds of those live in suburbs.[2] We are surrounded by more people than ever before in the history of our country. With these undeniable benefits in place, how could a Gallup Poll rank us among the loneliest people in the world?

Let's take a closer look at the story of Bob and Karen. Eight years ago Bob took a job at an office located in a growing suburb. Although this took them further from their families, both Bob and Karen had agreed that it would still be feasible to fly home on occasion because they were making more money and the airport was in close proximity to their house. Bob and Karen both rise at 6:30 A.M. Bob rushes to leave the house at 7:00 to beat the rush hour traffic; doing so allows him to get to work in thirty-five minutes as opposed to fifty-five minutes. He opens the door leading into the garage, hits the garage door opener, gets into his car, and pulls out of the driveway. He spots his new neighbor taking out the trash and waves to him with a forced smile on his face. As Bob drives down the street, he reminds himself that his *new* neighbor has been in the neighborhood now for two years, and he still can't remember his name. This thought lasts for about five seconds before the radio is turned on, and Bob's mind now turns to the matters of the day.

Karen has worked out an arrangement to be at work at 9:00 A.M. so she can drop off her two children at school at 8:15. There is the usual rush to get herself and the two children ready and out the door by 7:55, but on this day she manages to pull it off. With the same ritual precision, Karen makes her way to the car and starts heading out the driveway when one of the children announces that he has left a lunch inside. The easiest move for Karen would be to go back in through the front door, but she sees her next-door neighbor, one of the few retired people in the area, beginning her yard work for the day. While Karen would love to catch up with her elderly neighbor, she is afraid if they engage in a conversation the children will be late for school—and then she'll be late for work. So rather than risk being late, Karen makes her way back to the rear entry garage, opens the door with the automatic opener, and goes inside. As she grabs the forgotten lunch from the kitchen table, she realizes she has forgotten to set the security system. Once this is accomplished, off she goes again.

Bob and Karen encounter an average day at work—nine-and-a-half hours at the office, completing only four-and-a-half hours of real productive work. Both will bring home bulging briefcases, in the hopes of sneaking in another hour of work after the children are in bed. At 3:30, the children go to their after-school program and wait for Mom or Dad to pick them up.

It is 5:00 P.M., and Bob absolutely must leave the office if he is to pick up the children on time from the after-school program. As it often goes, Bob doesn't leave until 5:20, and he gets trapped in a ten-minute traffic jam because of a stalled car on the freeway. He arrives at the school thirty minutes late. Everyone is just a little edgy.

Bob and the kids pull into the rear entry garage at 6:15. Bob turns off the security system, ensuring that no one has tampered with their home while they have been gone. Karen arrives at 6:30. The first order of business is dinner. Bob and Karen agreed two years ago, with a little help from a family therapist, that with Karen's return to work to help pay the bills, sharing household chores was going to be a vital part of suburban life; Bob would need to share the load with her in the evenings.

While the children watch television, Mom and Dad are working together to heat up a tray of frozen lasagna and garlic bread. After dinner, the dishes are cleaned up, the mail is perused, homework papers are checked, and the children get ready for bed. It is now 9:00 P.M. The children are a half hour late getting to bed, but it was the best they could do. At 9:15 Bob and Karen finally sit down. They are exhausted, really too tired to talk, so the television gets beamed on, right in the middle of some prime-time drama. They both watch television until the news is over, look at their briefcases for a moment, and agree to let the work go undone. Finally, at 11:30, they make it to bed. A couple of words are exchanged, mostly businesslike talk concerning tomorrow's details. As they close their eyes, they both ponder how easy this day was. The remainder of the weeknights will be filled with sports practices, games, music lessons, and some evening meetings at the office.

The next day the family rises again to engage in what has become a way of life for five out of the seven days of their week. But now, the weekend has arrived!

Saturday and Sunday are used for three primary activities: house and lawn care, children's sports, and church. These activities take up most of the available hours, but on the average weekend there are a few hours of open time to be used for soaking in life with family and friends. The problem the Johnsons have is common for many other contemporary couples. First, their extended family members live in other cities around the United States. Second, they were so busy during the week they didn't make plans to do something with another family. Finally, while they would be open to spending some spontaneous time with the neighbors, no one is out in their front yards except a few men mowing their lawns with earphones wrapped securely around both ears and the companion radio strapped to their khaki-colored shorts. Everyone else is either away from home or safely sheltered inside their centrally air conditioned/heated homes, fully equipped with cable television or satellite dish—or if not inside the house, they're in their backyards, which are completely landscaped for privacy.

Occasionally an outing is planned with another couple or family who may live in another part of town. The time always seems to be a positive experience—yet, because few of the gatherings are routinely with the same family, neither Bob nor Karen feels comfortable sharing their deepest dreams and fears. Another weekend comes to a close with unvoiced stress and boredom, and Bob and Karen individually conclude that this was an unusual week; next week will be better. Well, eight years have now passed since they adopted their "American Dream" lifestyle, with somewhere around 416 weeks classified as "unusual."

Oh, there is one more important aspect to the Johnsons' life. Bob and Karen are Christians. They attend church just about every Sunday and have been involved in a church-sponsored small group for a little over a year. The group is made up of other couples of roughly the same age and meets in one of the members' homes every other week.

The Sunday worship services are usually uplifting and inspiring. Bob and Karen feel a sense of satisfaction with their children's involvement in the Sunday school program. As a matter of fact, it was their desire to give their children a religious and spiritual foundation that brought them back to church after a lapse during college and their early years of marriage. While the church is extremely friendly, the only people they really know are those who attend their small group.

The Johnsons' small group usually meets on the first and third Thursday night of each month from 7:00 to 9:30. The members of the group rotate the task of hosting the meeting in their homes. Most of the members live about ten to twenty minutes away from each other.

Bob and Karen joined the group in the hopes of finding a surrogate extended family, or at least a set of close friends with whom they could share their dreams and fears. After a year's worth of faithful attendance to the group, the Johnsons started to miss some of the meetings. Why? There were several

reasons. First, with their tight weekday schedule, it was difficult to eat dinner, check homework papers, bathe the children,
pick up a baby-sitter, drive to the small group get-together by
7:00, leave around 10:15, then take the baby-sitter back home,
and return home around 11:30. This routine simply exhausted
this couple, who were in search of meaningful friendships and
a sense of personal peace.

A second reason the priority for the small group
diminished was the children's sports games and practices.
Both children play soccer and baseball—and one or both
of the children have either a practice or a game on
Thursday night.

A third reason was the disappointment the Johnsons
were feeling over how seldom the members of the group
got together outside of the regularly scheduled meetings.
There seemed to be a mutual desire on everyone's part to
get together, but something always seemed to prevent a
more relaxed and spontaneous outing. Because the group
only saw each other for a few hours twice (sometimes only
once) a month, there wasn't the sense of intimacy the
Johnsons wanted in order to feel free to really share their
dreams and fears. While they would consider their small
group members to be their closest friends, the Johnsons
were longing for something more.

To look at the outside shell of the Johnsons' life, it
would appear they have it all together, yet on the inside
they are two of the statistically lonely people of whom
George Gallup writes. Bob and Karen are just two of the
millions of Americans who are searching to belong.
Moreover, what is true of the Johnson family is intensified

in the single-parent home. The activity for the adult parent is usually doubled, practically eliminating any time for the development of personal relationships. In addition, the single parent often has to burn a great deal of additional energy negotiating with the blended family members.

The single adult is not exempt from loneliness either. While more time can be allocated to enhancing adult relationships instead of managing children's activities, the additional time still leaves them at home many hours feeling deeply alone. While there is usually an active group of acquaintances, most singles still long for a deeper companionship than what seems to be in their grasp. One of the most significant struggles for a single person living in suburban America is the lack of wholesome gathering spots for singles. The lack of access to community means that isolation rules.

The purpose of this book is to help people who feel like the Johnsons find what they are searching for—to help people discover a rich sense of *community*. To belong! In our journey of discovery, we will explore three obstacles that hinder our attainment of biblical community in America. Three comprehensive and practical solutions will be offered to overcome these obstacles; these solutions will be more specifically defined in the fifteen characteristics that must be present in order for community to be experienced. The promise of this book is that restructuring our lifestyles around these fifteen characteristics will fulfill our "search to belong" and give us the rich, enduring fellowship we were created by God to experience.

"More than any other book I've read, *The Connecting Church* describes and defines what spiritual community is and tells us how to do it."—**LARRY CRABB**, author, *The Safest Place on Earth*

The development of meaningful relationships, where every member carries a significant sense of belonging, is central to what it means to be the church. So why do many Christians feel disappointed and disillusioned with their efforts to experience authentic community? Despite the best efforts of pastors, small group leaders, and faithful laypersons, church too often is a place of loneliness rather than connection.

Church can be so much better. So intimate and alive. *The Connecting Church* tells you how. The answer may seem radical today, but it was a central component of life in the early church. First-century Christians knew what it meant to live in vital community with one another, relating with a depth and commitment that made "the body of Christ" a perfect metaphor for the church. What would it take to reclaim that kind of love, joy, support, and dynamic spiritual growth? Read this book and find out.

——— PRAISE FOR *THE CONNECTING CHURCH* ———

"This is by far the best corporate plan for spiritual formation and growth that I know of in a contemporary setting."

DALLAS WILLARD
Author, *The Divine Conspiracy* and *The Spirit of the Disciplines*

"Randy Frazee's thinking will help to transform our churches into authentic communities."

KEN BLANCHARD
Coauthor, *The One Minute Manager* and *Leadership by the Book*

"Overcoming the isolation of individuals is an urgent task for churches. This progress report from a Texas church that is finding a way to do it may have landmark status. Pastoral strategists cannot afford not to read it, for it sets out a plan that works."

J. I. PACKER
Author, *Knowing God*

"This book points the way to desperately needed Christian community that touches the soul at a deeper level."

MARSHALL SHELLEY
Editor, *Leadership Journal*

"Randy Frazee is an out-of-the-box leader whose way of thinking is exactly what the 21st century church needs to effectively do the work of God's kingdom. Listen to what he says!"

JOHN C. MAXWELL
Founder, The INJOY Group

Cover design: Tobias Design
CHURCH AND MINISTRY / CHURCH LIFE / CHURCH GROWTH

US $16.99/$25.50 CAN
ISBN 0-310-23308-9

51699
9 780310 233084
EAN

ZONDERVAN™
WWW.ZONDERVAN.COM

WILLOW CREEK
RESOURCES
www.willowcreek.com

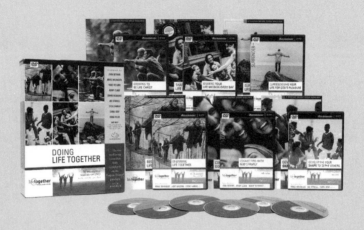

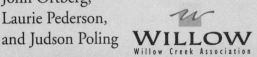

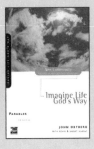

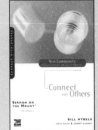

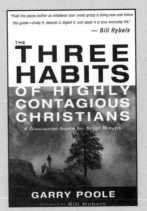

SPECIAL OFFER

Celebrating Friendship	0-310-21338-X
Discovering Your Spiritual Gifts	0-310-21340-1
Embracing Forgiveness	0-310-21341-X
Experiencing God's Presence	0-310-21343-6
Finding Joy	0-310-21336-3
Growing in Prayer	0-310-21335-5
Knowing God's Will	0-310-21339-8
Strengthening Your Faith	0-310-21337-1

SPECIAL OFFER

Becoming a Woman God Can Use: A Study on Ester	0-310-24782-9
Choosing the Joy of Obedience: A Study on Mary	0-310-24784-5
Daring to Be Different: A Study on Deborah	0-310-24781-0
Entrusting Your Dreams to God: A Study on Hannah	0-310-24783-7
Facing Life's Uncertainties: A Study on Sarah	0-310-24786-1
Trusting That God Will Provide: A Study on Ruth	0-310-24785-3

SPECIAL OFFER

see below for details

Old Testament Challenge –Kit 1	0-310-24891-4
OTC 1: Teaching Guide	0-310-24892-2
OTC 1: Discussion Guide	0-310-24893-0
Old Testament Challenge –Kit 2	0-310-24931-7
OTC 2: Teaching Guide	0-310-24932-5
OTC 2: Discussion Guide	0-310-24933-3
Old Testament Challenge –Kit 3	0-310-25031-5
OTC 3: Teaching Guide	0-310-25032-3
OTC 3: Discussion Guide	0-310-25033-1
Old Testament Challenge –Kit 4	0-310-25142-7
OTC 4: Teaching Guide	0-310-25143-5
OTC 4: Discussion Guide	0-310-25144-3
OTC Implementation Guide	0-310-24939-2
Taking the Old Testament Challenge	0-310-24913-9

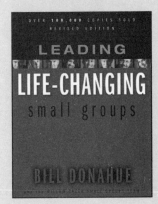

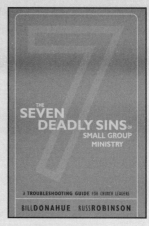

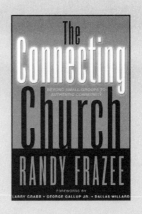

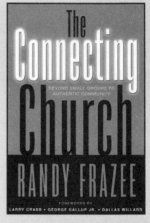

We want to hear from you. Please send your comments about this
book to us in care of zreview@zondervan.com. Thank you.

GRAND RAPIDS, MICHIGAN 49530 USA

WWW.ZONDERVAN.COM